THE WALKER

THE UNTOLD STORY
OF BLACK BART

Happy Birthday Gary !

Enjoy !

— Bruce Bradley

BY
BRUCE BRADLEY

Published in the United States by

The Pretlow Group, Ltd.

THE WALKER

Also by Bruce Bradley:

HUGH GLASS

THE LAST JAGUAR

DRELLIKS

THE SEEDS OF DARKNESS

THE TRIBE

25 THINGS YOU SHOULD KNOW ABOUT WINE

For James Reader's

great-grandson—Fred Langdon—and
Fred's wife, Patty

ACKNOWLEDGEMENTS:

I wish to thank Mike Blanton and Jeff Hansen for their help in editing this book, Susan Goldstein and Sylvia Rowan of the San Francisco History Center and Public Library, for their help in researching The Nevada House, David and Marguerite Baxley of the Doris Foley Historical Research Library in Nevada City for their help in finding the articles about Charley and James Reader, Lynn Woodward of blackbart.com, Malcolm E. Barker of Londonborn Books for letting me use the article "I Was Buried In Complete Darkness", Fred Langdon for showing me where Charley's cabin used to sit out at the Reader Ranch, and a very special thanks to Charley's great-great grandchildren, Billy Reames and Tiffany Derrick, for taking the time to talk with me. I would also like to thank Wells Fargo for the use of their photos of Charley, as well as the Army Corps of Engineers for their maps of the Civil War battles that Charley took part in.

And a special thanks to Kevin R. Sweeney for his cover art!

Thanks to you all!

Charles Earl Boles—AKA Black Bart (1829—?)

(Photo courtesy of Wells Fargo)

DEAR READER, this book is a work of fiction, but a great deal of what lies within these pages, the people, places and events, were real. Charley, his cousin David and brother Robert were of course, all real. The events that took place aboard the paddle wheeler *Zanesville* were real and were recorded in G.W. Thissell's book "Crossing The Plains In '49". The killing of the Pawnee squaw and its aftermath came from an undocumented account I ran across while researching the Pawnee Indians for "Hugh Glass". Likewise, the men I described from the 116th Illinois Infantry Regiment and the battles they took part in were also all real.

Nearly every small town in northern California has a local legend concerning Black Bart—and deservedly so. Charley traveled far and wide when committing his robberies, all the way from Jackson County, Oregon to central California and covering almost every county in the northern part of the state. And in nearly every one of those counties, it seemed he was known by a different name.

The National Hotel in Nevada City, CA is still in operation and is the oldest continuously operating hotel west of the Rocky Mountains.

The 900-acre Reader Ranch is still an operating cattle ranch and is owned by James Reader's great-grandchildren. The Nevada House, at 132 6th Street, in San Francisco, CA was owned by the Lee family until its collapse in the 1906 San Francisco earthquake.

In 1854 Charley married Mary Elizabeth Johnson. They had three daughters prior to the Civil War and one son after.

And of course, the 28 robberies that Charley admitted to were also real, although I personally believe there may have been a few more that he intentionally left out...

Enjoy!

Bruce Bradley
April 2017

THE WALKER

ONE

I AM OLD now, far older than many thought these bones would ever get to be. One thing I have learned in my life is that, in nearly every situation that you may face, there are two roads. One road leads to power, the other, away. Many people think they know me, from having read of things I've done. I find it amusing that, of the current friends and neighbors I have, not one knows of the things I once did, or why, or of who I once was…

When I was two years old, my family moved from Norfolk, England to America. I remember nothing of that crossing. My first memories are of living on our farm in Jefferson County, New York. They are, for the most part, good memories—my mother, cleaning and cooking; me, playing in the yard or out in the fields with kids from nearby farms, my father coming in from working our farm and dinners around the table with my family. My father had a gentle patience about him and, although he never claimed it, a quality that spoke of nobility. Some have said that I inherited that. It may cause some who think they know me now to laugh, but from my father I learned the importance of honesty, hard work, integrity and a sense of justice. From my mother, I learned manners, how to read and write, and an indefinable quality she called 'grace'. My memories of that time of my life are good ones. I was the seventh out of nine children—six boys and three girls. My older brothers protected me from the local bullies and taught me to wrestle, which in time I became better at than they. For a time, I was known as the best collar and elbow wrestler in Jefferson County. Those lessons served me well. On a number of occasions, during the war, knowing how to wrestle saved my life.

When I was six I contracted smallpox and nearly died. I survived, and my mother often said it was because God was saving me for something greater. I find subtle humor in that, these days.

People have often said that I'm afraid of horses. That isn't completely true. I don't trust horses and they seem to sense it. I've tried to change that a couple of times, but it's too deep inside me. Horses, like dogs, have uncanny instincts. Every time I tried to befriend a horse it would shy away from me, so it's something I've learned to live with. I do like dogs.

When I was nine years old there was this girl, Cassie Frye. Cassie was two years older than me and the prettiest thing you ever saw, and we were friends. Truth is, at the ripe, old age of nine, I was sweet on her. One day I was in town. I happened to look across the street and there she was. She looked up at the same time and, smiling, started to cross the street. She was wearing a bonnet, which must have limited her vision. She never saw the runaway wagon. When I yelled at her she just stopped. Two of the four horses went over her. The image of the hoofprints they left on her pretty blue dress is something I've never been able to erase from my memory.

I know it's wrong to blame all horses for the accidental actions of only two, but it's there and I've never been able to shake it.

My father tried to teach me to be a farmer, but it never really took. In 1849 I was twenty years old. News came of a huge gold strike in California. Half the people in America seemed to have caught gold fever, and I was one of them. My cousin David and I joined up with three other young men and headed west. In mid-March we boarded the steamer *Zanesville* in Muskingum, Ohio, headed for St. Louis, which was the jumping-off spot for anyone headed for California.

The energy aboard the boat was incredible. Whole families had sold their property and belongings for a stake that would get them to the gold fields. We watched the big paddle-wheel as it churned the waters of the Muskingum River, sending a light spray into the air. Despite the chill, the spray felt good. I watched the people lining the docks, many teary-eyed from their goodbyes, grow smaller as the steamer headed out into the center of the river.

The excitement of gold fever ran all along the decks of the ship, almost a living thing. Standing next to me at the rail, Henry Albright found it impossible to keep still.

"Think of it—California! We're finally on our way! We're going to be rich, Charley, I can feel it!"

"You have to get there first, Henry," cousin David said dryly. "Then you have to find the gold."

"We will, David! We will. Before it's over, every one of us will probably be wealthy beyond our dreams!"

"Maybe, if we don't get killed by Indians or God-knows-what along the way first."

"We'll be fine. You'll see."

"I hope you're right," David told him.

The people waving from shore had become tiny, almost too small to see. I moved away from the rail, happy to be under way. I hadn't joined in with the conversation, but I was as excited about going as Henry was. I also knew David was right. We had a lot of hardship to face before we got to the gold fields. Somehow, I was eager for that, too. The Great Unknown had called to me—to all of us, and we had answered. The five of us, me, David, Henry and James and

Carl Roberts had joined forces. We had pooled our money, formed a pact and were determined to make it to California and strike it rich. Despite David's misgivings, I knew he was just as excited as the rest of us. The gold fever ran high. Few could resist it.

The *Zanesville* had originally been called *The Zanesville Packet*. It was built for river travel in 1843, then decommissioned in 1846. Three years later, the great rush for the gold fields brought the demand for riverboats to an all-time high and brought the *Zanesville* out of retirement. She was a stately, 88-ton paddle-wheeler. I wondered why she was ever retired in the first place.

No sooner had we gotten underway, than the great paddle-wheeler slowed once more to a stop. A short while later the *Zanesville* entered the first of a series of locks that we would have to pass through to get to the Missouri River. All in all, there were eleven locks, supported by ten dams and covering a 112-mile stretch of the Muskingum River. The system had opened eight years earlier, in 1841, enabling the Muskingum to become the main waterway in Ohio and a major thoroughfare for river traffic.

Once we were inside the lock, the gate closed and, after a short delay, the lock began to drain. The *Zanesville's* deckhands kept her stationary during this time, using ropes that had been thrown to them from shore. Although I had heard of this type of river travel, this was my first time to be inside one of the locks. I found it interesting.

Once the water level in the lock had gone down several feet, the second gate opened and we were allowed to proceed on our way once more. I continued on my tour about the deck of the boat. When I reached the aft section I stood for several moments, regarding the great paddle-wheel and marveling at the unending ingenuity of man. After some moments of this I turned to go—and immediately had a collision.

The young woman I had collided with fell back, startled and angered by my clumsiness. The scent of her perfume—*lilac*, I think— brushed past my nose.

"*Sir*!" she began. "Do you not think you should watch where you are going?"

"I'm sorry miss, I—" I stopped, momentarily unable to continue. The young woman I had bumped into was exceedingly lovely. Her long brown hair was curled and fell to one side, down across her breast. Her dark eyes had a fire in them that stole my words away. She was, perhaps, a little on the plump side, but that in no way detracted from her beauty.

"You what—?" She demanded.

"I—I was captivated watching the paddle wheel. When I turned to go I did not see you. Please forgive me."

"Well...I suppose no harm was done, but you should pay better attention next time!"

"I promise," I told her. Then; "Charles Earl Bowles at your service. My friends call me Charley."

"Pleased, I'm sure," she said without looking at me. Nor did she offer me her name.

"Are you...for the gold country?" I prodded.

Now she looked at me.

"Yes," she said. "My father and I are headed there. You?"

"Yes, I am. My friends and I are going prospecting. We've formed a company," I lied.

"Well, good luck to you and your friends, Mr. Bowles." She turned to go.

"It's Charley," I told her.

"Yes, well, good luck."

"Perhaps we'll bump into one another again..."

She turned back and gave me a shocked look.

"I...meant that figuratively, of course."

She continued to stare at me for a moment. Then she nodded, slowly.

"Of course." Then she was gone, down the passageway, leaving behind only the subtle hint of lilac to remind me of her former presence.

Well, Bowles, I thought to myself, *never let it be said that you don't have a way with women. It's probably a <u>bad</u> way, but it's a way...*

I moved off, still thinking of the young woman. I continued to think of her for some time after that, and kept hoping for a glimpse of her and the chance to speak with her again. Little could I know then that I would, in fact, see her again before we reached St. Louis, but that I would scarcely recognize her, for so changed would she be.

TWO

NIGHTIME ABOARD the *Zanesville* was a time of merriment and magic. The river wove its own spell, while the extreme enthusiasm of those of us on board made it seem that anything was possible. A band played in the main salon—sedately during dinner, then livelier after the tables had all been cleared. There was dancing, but neither I nor my friends joined into it. I *might* have been tempted into it, had I again encountered that lovely young woman with the dark and beautifully angry eyes, but she was nowhere about. Once, I thought I caught a hint of lilac, but it wasn't her.

The river and the lure of gold attracted every sort of person—not all of them honest. The five of us had banded together. We had combined our resources and agreed to spend nothing without group consent. We hoped this would save us from those who would prey on the unwary, but others were not so lucky. I remember seeing one man, early in the evening. He was as excited as we were about hitting the gold fields, perhaps more so. Later on, that first evening, I saw him standing at the rail, looking desolate. He had lost his entire stake in a poker game. Now he had no choice but to return home and resume his former life. I vowed then and there that this would not happen to me. No matter what, I would not turn back and go home—not until I had reached California and worked in the gold fields. Starve I might, or die at the hands of savages, but I would not go back. My pride was too strong to allow it.

I awoke, just before daybreak, to a buzz of activity in the corridor outside our cabin. I rose from my bunk and dressed as silently as I could, too excited to remain in bed. Quietly then, so as not to wake the others, I slipped out of the room. The rich, warm aroma of coffee struck me immediately as a steward walked by carrying a tray with a pot on it. The smell caused my stomach to growl. I headed for the main salon. A short while later, with a pastry and a hot mug in hand, I watched the sun come up over the banks of the Muskingum.

It was a beautiful morning. I felt alive and vibrant with enthusiasm. Gold—and the thrill of adventure lay before me, filling the days ahead with excitement I had never before known.

Not many people were up, but the stewards were already busy. Draining what was left of my coffee, I headed back to the salon for a refill. I turned a corner and encountered two stewards who were having a heated conversation. I heard the words:

"—Spread like wildfire! No one is to hear of this, understand? No one!"

The two looked up sharply in my direction, then back at each other.

"Remember what I told you!" The man who had been speaking hissed. Then the two moved quickly away.

Before many hours had passed, it would become all too clear what they had been attempting to conceal.

One by one, my companions rose and came out on deck—the last being Henry Albright. My cousin David, never one to miss an opportunity at criticism, pointed the fact out to all who were near.

"Aha!" David exclaimed. "The *slugabed* finally arises!"

"What? Slugabed? Me?" Henry answered. "Is this a workday, that I have to account for my sleeping habits?"

"No," David told him. "I was just pointing out that you *were* the last one to rise—"

Henry shrugged as if to say, "So?"

"You didn't beat him by that much, David," I interjected.

"No, but beat him I did."

A sudden commotion diverted our attention. Some people rushed past us—a man and two women. One of the women was helping the other along. I recognized the woman who was being helped. It was an older woman, Mrs. Putman. I'd spoken briefly with her and her husband when I came on board. They were from Zanesville.

Mrs. Putman looked *very* upset.

"Mrs. Putman!" I said as they went past. "Is everything all right? Is there anything I might do to help?"

They stopped and looked at me. Mrs. Putman seemed on the verge of collapse. The younger woman with her was fighting to hold her up.

Mrs. Putman looked at me and shook her head.

"There's nothing to be done," she said mournfully. "It's James. He's gone! Cholera took him in the night!"

With that, the three of them turned and ushered off down the passageway, leaving my friends and I to ponder her words and what they indicated.

Cholera. James Putman had been the first to die.

He would be, by far, not the last.

By the time we reached Louisville, Kentucky—scarcely a quarter of the distance of our 500-mile journey—three more people had succumbed to the dreaded disease. We put the dead off at Louisville and continued on our way.

Just as the steward said, the Cholera spread like wildfire. It struck quickly, and its effects were terrible to behold. People we saw who were smiling and happy at breakfast were taken ill before lunchtime and dead before supper. We moved about the *Zanesville* carefully, kerchiefs held tightly over our noses and mouths in an effort to ward off the smells of vomit and diarrhea, and after the first day, decaying flesh. I spent as much time forward as I could, letting the damp spray that came over the bow cover my face and dampen my jacket, and drive the bad smells behind me.

In the end, I did not spend enough time there.

At one point, as I was moving from my berth to the bow of the boat, a young woman rushed out of her cabin and brushed me aside in an effort to make it to the rail to vomit. I stopped and watched her for a moment, completely unwilling to participate in her wretchedness, but unable to turn away.

When she was finished, she turned back and looked at me, saying nothing as she wiped the corner of her mouth with an unsteady hand while holding onto the rail with the other. Something about her was familiar... Then I caught the scent of lilac, mixed with the stench of vomit. My mouth dropped open as I realized that this was the bright young woman I had encountered before. She was completely changed. The plumpness of her was gone, replaced by hollow, sunken cheeks and lips were bluish in hue. She looked far older than she had two days earlier. She looked like death.

Embarrassed and somewhat shaken, I gave a slight bow and turned away.

I never saw that young woman again. The deckhands, those who weren't too ill to work themselves, began to pile the deceased out on the stern deck, so that the smell would be carried off in our wake. Just before we reached St. Louis, we docked long enough to offload nine more dead. I have no way of knowing if that young woman was among them, but I think perhaps she was.

And to this day, I cannot be near someone wearing lilac scent without becoming physically ill.

The loss of thirteen people who had started the trip with us shook everyone aboard the *Zanesville*. We had only begun our journey. To have so many taken so quickly and in such a frightful way sobered us all. The treatment of those who died did nothing to abate our misgivings, for the nine who were taken off twenty miles from St. Louis were all buried in a common grave. No marker of any kind was left to record their passing or who, in life, they had been.

St. Louis was a sight! The wharf was crowded with people, all pressed together and eager to get started for the gold country. My companions and I left the *Zanesville* and were informed that it would be two full days before we could get passage up the Missouri River to St. Joseph. We busied ourselves gathering supplies for our trip, including a four-horse wagon in which the five of us slept while waiting for the next boat. It had no proper cover as yet, but we managed to string a canvas that enclosed us nicely. It was pretty tight quarters, but it beat the alternative of sleeping outside in the damp and cold.

For that two days, we stayed together as a group and were careful not to lose sight of one another, for a man alone would be an easy target for any kind of foul play. We had all heard stories of hapless travelers who had been unwary. Each of us, at one point or another, was approached by someone seeking to tempt us into a game, or a plan, or a scheme to get rich quickly. Fortunately for us, we managed to avoid them all. It was an exciting time and place, true, and people of all sorts *were* getting rich, but we had our own plan and were resolved to stick to it.

When, at last, we boarded the *Winfield Scott* and began steaming up the Missouri River toward St. Joseph, I breathed a sigh of relief. So far, at least, we were all intact.

But that wouldn't last either.

The river was running higher than normal, even for this time of year. Everywhere we looked there was flooding. Each high spot became an island unto itself. Most were cramped with horses, hogs, sheep and cattle that were trying to escape the rising water and were, undoubtedly, starving to death.

"It seems like someone would do something," Henry said.

I agreed with him.

"I know. If a man had a big boat, or could hire a big boat and go 'round collecting all that livestock, he could do pretty well for himself."

"Bad idea, Charley," David interjected. "They *hang* men for taking other people's livestock."

"That wouldn't be rustling," I told him. "It's rescue."

"Would you bet your life on that?"

"Anyway," I said, ignoring him, "you could sell them back to the farmers for, say, thirty percent more than it cost you to go get them.

You'd still make a handsome profit, and you'd be doing a service to humanity."

"And what if the farmer couldn't pay—or refused to pay? You couldn't keep the livestock and you couldn't sell it. In the end, you'd lose your shirt—or worse!"

"Well…I still think there is a way to make it work. Think of the poor animals! If they're left there, they'll die!"

"Better them than you, Charley. That's what I say. Better them than you."

We continued upriver. When we reached St. Joseph it was raining heavily and was bitterly cold. Passengers aboard the *Winfield Scott* were anxious to leave the boat and find shelter, many of us soaked through with rain and shivering uncontrollably. We pushed and shoved, pressing to get off the boat with all the good sense of stampeding cattle. Ten feet ahead of me one old Dutchman took a spill right off the gangplank and into the icy water. He splashed awkwardly below us as his wife yelled in a panic, "He can't swim! He can't swim!" That slowed the throng long enough for some of the men ahead of me to pull him from the water. The poor man looked deathly miserable and there was nowhere to go for comfort. As I passed by I heard him say to his wife:

"Mine Gott, I vish I vas at home!"

Our wagon and our supplies were off-loaded unceremoniously onto the dock. Hastily, we loaded our supplies into the wagon. We had a years' worth of beans, rice, sugar, coffee and flour, all of which had to be kept from moisture. We packed them as best we could in the false bottom of the wagon. Then, in the midst of a rainstorm, we set about putting the cover on the wagon. It took some doing, but once we had it up we felt secure.

Despite the rain, St. Joseph was in a state of frenzy. Men rushed to and about, looking for supplies and livestock—horses, mules or oxen to pull their wagons to the gold country. We were no different, for a wagon to get us to the gold country would be no good without oxen or horses to pull it.

Days passed, turning into weeks. We were waiting for the weather to clear so that we could get moving, as well as a train to form with someone to lead the way. This was a long and dangerous journey we were all undertaking. Striking off alone was foolhardy and ill-advised. Yet, there were those who did, their patience worn thin by the long delays. How many of those actually made it to California I could not begin to say. Still others became disheartened, sold their gear and went home. We weren't among them, but we weren't unscathed, either.

Cholera and Winter Fever were ever-present. Many who were eager to start for California died without ever setting foot on the trail. One morning I awoke feeling out of sorts, a scratchiness in the back of my throat. A short while later I began to shiver and could not stop. By sundown I was burning up with fever.

I remember little of the days that followed. I do remember my cousin, David, trying to feed me water, and me spitting it out.

"I can't drink that," I told him. "It's brackish!"

"It's only got a pinch of salt in it," David answered. "It's something I learned from my Mother, Charley. *Drink it!* It may save your life!"

I did as David asked, although the taste of it seemed only to add to my misery.

I know not how many days the fever raged within me. One morning I woke up and realized that I was no longer within the confines of the wagon. I was in a hospital. My cousin was there, too. The others were gone. It seemed the opportunity to leave for California came while I was too ill to travel. Henry, James and Carl had gone on without us.

It was nearly a month before I was strong enough to leave the hospital. The fever, while having broken, returned again and again before finally leaving me to recover. By the time I was well enough to travel it was nearly June. No trains would be starting for California this late into the season for fear of being trapped by early snows when Fall came. This meant David and I would have to wait until the following Spring before we could start again.

True to my promise to myself, David and I did not return home. We spent a harsh winter in St. Joseph. Both of us managed to find jobs—David found work as a clerk in a store. I got a job in a sawmill. We saved every penny we could and, in April of 1850, headed out once more.

THREE

THAT FIRST trip across the plains to California is a story in itself. Nothing could have prepared us for what we were to face—the vastness of the plains, the endless days of walking, the monotony... David and I fell in with two other young men—Mathew Kinneson and Jack Kenner. They were good, solid lads and we all got along well. We had a good leader, Captain Hallowell, who had been over the trail thrice before and had led two trains of wagons prior to taking us on. Occasionally, there would be some excitement, but Captain Hallowell always seemed to know what to do and how to handle it. Nothing seemed to rile or upset him, which gave us all confidence that we would make it through. We had all heard stories of the Donner Party, four years earlier, who had become trapped by snow on the eastern side of the Sierra Nevada mountains. Some of the party had died from starvation, and those who didn't had been forced to revert to cannibalism to survive. Captain Hallowell assured us that we had left early enough and were making decent time, and that we would be in California well ahead of the snows.

There is one incident that I will tell you about, which affected us all deeply and put a dark cloud over the days that followed. There was this young man, Otto Herrington. Otto was a little younger than I was, in his late teens. He had an air about him, a sort of arrogance. He traveled with his family and fashioned himself a hunter. For Otto, being a hunter meant shooting anything that moved. Oh, he did provide occasional meat for his table, but he also shot birds, snakes, lizards—and would usually leave them where they lay. For six weeks he bragged that he would "—shoot the first Indian I see!" One afternoon he made the brag again. A short while later we happened to pass by an Indian woman, who turned out to be Pawnee squaw. My cousin David, sick as the rest of us of Otto's bragging, made the comment: "There's an Indian…"

Without a word Otto looked at the woman, took aim and shot her dead.

You could have poured iced water over me. David was horrified. He looked at Otto with hot anger and contempt.

"You insufferable ass!" he yelled. "You've killed her!"

Otto merely made a face and shrugged as if to say, "So what?"

Several of us ran to try to help the woman, but she was quite dead, shot through the heart. Many things Otto might have been, but he was a good shot.

The following morning, a short while before noon, we found our wagons surrounded by more than one hundred Pawnee warriors, and they were ready for war.

Captain Hallowell remained calm as always, but his face showed grave concern. He walked out to meet them.

The Pawnee chief rode forward. He was both ancient and magnificent. His eyes burned with anger. He did not speak English, but one of his warriors did. The chief spoke and the warrior translated.

"You kill squaw! Why?" he demanded.

Captain Hallowell knew of the shooting—he had to, as it had been the talk of the camp the night before and Otto had been severely chastised for it. At first, Hallowell tried feigning ignorance.

"What squaw? When?"

"Last day! Give us one who kill!"

"Where? What are you talking about?"

"Give us one who kill! Now, or we go war! You die! Man, woman, babies—all die!"

Captain Hallowell knew he was beaten. He nodded once and sighed heavily in defeat. Without turning his back to the Indians, he spoke loudly to us.

"Who killed the Indian woman?" he asked.

All eyes were on Otto, who stood holding his rifle and looking at the ground. Finally, he lifted his head.

"I did!" he said defiantly.

Instantly, two warriors rode to where Otto stood. Otto raised his rifle to shoot.

"Don't fight them, you fool!" Captain Hallowell yelled. "You'll have us all killed!"

Otto relaxed his grip on the rifle. The two Indians dismounted and jerked it from his hands. They then took his arms. One of them kicked him behind the knee, forcing him to the ground, where they bound his hands behind him. They then jerked him to his feet and led him away. The Pawnee chief sat on his horse, unmoving, glaring at Captain Hallowell. Finally, he spoke to his translator.

"Chief say you stay, watch, listen," the man said. Captain Hallowell stared back at them, gravely concerned but unmoving. The chief and his translator then pulled back and joined the others.

The Indians took Otto to a nearby stand of trees. They tied Otto to one of the trees, cut away his clothes and built a fire. Some of them began chanting, dancing and giving out yips and yells. There were too many of the Indians around

Otto for us to see what was going on, but we could hear.

For the next five hours we listened to Otto's awful, tortured screams. These were offset by the agonized wailing of his mother and sisters. Otto's father was beside himself.

"Damnit Hallowell! We have to do something! That is my boy they're torturing!"

Captain Hallowell shook his head. "There is nothing to be done, Friedrich," he said. "Your boy took the life of one of their women. It was a man's decision and, God help him, he's paying a man's price for it. There is nothing we can do—they outnumber us two to one and they are all seasoned warriors. If we try to fight, you, your wife and your daughters will all die, and the rest of us as well! *Nothing* good can come of it! We do not have a *choice* here!"

Mr. Harrington seemed to shrink in upon himself. He backed away, buried his face in his hands and said plaintively, "My God, please! Help my boy! Help my Otto…!"

The afternoon wore on. The faces of many of the men and women were ashen with fear. Some were near panic. Others were outraged and wanted to fight. Only Captain Hallowell's quiet courage and determination kept us all together. For the first time, I realized what my mother had been talking about when she spoke of "grace". I am absolutely certain that it was Hallowell's courage and grace that kept us alive that day.

It would be a week before I was able to get up the courage to bring that day up to him. I asked him how he had managed to remain unafraid in a situation that could easily have meant the death of us all.

"Oh, I was afraid, all right. But Charley, I learned something long ago, and it's helped me get through more than one tight spot—and that is that fear isn't real. It seems like a real thing, but it isn't. Fear is a reaction we have to a certain situation. If you can remember that when things get tight, it'll help you keep control, and maybe save your life."

Toward the end of the afternoon, Otto's screaming became more and more shrill. Then, abruptly, it stopped. Minutes later the Indians mounted their horses and left.

By now it was nearly dusk. We ran to the stand of trees to see if there was anything that we could do, but Otto was gone.

I've seen many horrible things in my life, but there is little to compare with the sight of a man who has been tied to a tree, scalped, and then skinned alive.

FOUR

WHAT HAD happened to Otto affected us all deeply, especially David. In a way, it forced us in a very sobering manner to acknowledge the dangers that we all faced on this trip. A sarcastic challenge from my cousin and a callous response from Otto could easily have meant the death of us all. In the days that followed we moved at our usual pace, but our awareness had changed. We were all a little less cocky and a little more serious about what we were doing.

We buried Otto out on a low hill, under a cottonwood tree. We marked his grave with a wooden cross, and moved on.

Occasionally, after that, we would see Indians. At those times, my hand would always seek out my rifle.

"It's not usually the ones you see that you have to worry about" Captain Hallowell said. "They're letting us see them. It's when you don't see them, that you need to worry."

Little by little, the Rocky Mountains began to grow before us. In July, they loomed over us like some impassible barrier. I had heard of "the elephant" and now I thought I knew what people were talking about. Those mountains seemed impossibly high and imposing. The sight of them was daunting. I was sure this had to be the elephant people talked about. I was wrong.

"Don't worry, Charley," Captain Hallowell told me. "This isn't the elephant. We'll be taking the South Pass. It's uphill, but it isn't horrible." Then he added, "The elephant is still ahead of us, waiting."

For days, we traveled steadily uphill. Then the way before us seemed nearly to level out. We passed through a saddle between the mountains and the going was actually easier than it had been before.

"This is the South Pass I told you about," Hallowell said to me. "See? It isn't bad at all."

In early September, we finally met "the elephant". We were at a place called "Roller Pass", which lay south of where the Donner Party had become trapped. Our oxen and horses were unhitched and taken separately to the top of a long and very steep hill. When I say long, I mean hundreds and hundreds of feet. Upon first seeing it I was struck with an unreasoning fear. I thought, *This just isn't possible!*

Each wagon had to be pulled up the hill alone. At the top of the hill, logs had been set in place to act as rollers, to prevent friction—hence the name "Roller Pass". Dangerous as this was, it was far preferable to lifting the wagons up the cliffs, as had been done years earlier. Somehow, we managed to make it up that steep slope. The panic I had felt upon seeing the pass was replaced by elation as I realized that I was now looking down into California. We had made it—we were at the end of our journey.

Finally, we had made it across the Sierra Nevada mountains. We stopped at Illinoistown, which years later would later be called Colfax, after the railroad went in. David and I wasted no time and were soon working our own claim, out on the north fork of the American River, about fifteen miles from the town.

In all my days I had never imagined living in a place as beautiful as this. Granite rocks the size of a small cabin, magnificent pines, the fresh, almost overpowering scent of cedar—and fish that would practically jump onto your hook. It was a paradise.

Anyone who tells you that placer mining is anything but hard work is selling you something. The days are long and back-breaking, and that water is barely this side of freezing, but the chance of hitting a big strike was a real, physical thing. We had some luck right out of the gate and that gave us hope that kept us moving forward. We *should* have built shelter for us right off, but we were so eager to find gold that we lived in a tent—until it was nearly too late. October gave us a dose of reality. We stopped long enough to lay a crude foundation for a cabin. After that I worked at building it, while David continued to work the claim. Carpentry I had learned from my father, working on the farm, and I had worked in a sawmill, so it seemed I was the natural choice to be the one to build it. We vastly overpaid for a small woodstove and I barely got the cabin finished before the rains and the snow hit us. We hadn't taken the time to lay up a supply of firewood, so even with the woodstove, we spent a fairly miserable winter.

Occasionally, we would trudge into town. Those were high points for us. We were able to get word of what was going on in the outside world, read a newspaper, or buy an occasional book. Both David and I could read, so we took turns reading to each other. That and only that made the days when we were cooped up in the cabin tolerable.

I could not help but notice that a change had come over David. He had always been sarcastic and superior, proud of his rapier-like wit that kept everyone around him on their toes. Now he seemed quiet and withdrawn. One afternoon I returned to the cabin, after foraging for firewood, and found him sitting quietly, tear-tracks streaming down his face. I asked him what was wrong.

"It was all my fault, Charley. All my fault. Otto—that Indian woman—they would both be alive if I had just kept my mouth shut. I couldn't—!"

"David," I told him, "you couldn't have known. You couldn't have *known*! Otto was an arrogant young fool, but none of us would have thought he would kill that woman. He brought all of that on himself, no matter what you said!"

"Maybe, but I can't help but think that if I'd just kept quiet—if I hadn't tried to call his bluff—that Indian woman would still be alive, and so would Otto... And God, Charley, what a horrible, *horrible* way to die!"

"You can't know that you caused that, cousin. You cannot know that. Stop whipping yourself."

David nodded, but guilt would continue to haunt him.

Christmas in Illinoistown was a festive event. There was a big celebration in town and all the miners, including David and I, went to it. I gave David a large Bowie knife—named after Jim Bowie, who had died at the Alamo fourteen years earlier—and David gave me a Cree tomahawk he had traded for. I carried that tomahawk for years, until I lost it at the Battle of Arkansas Post. It served me well.

Back at the cabin, both David and I admitted how horribly homesick we both were. This was the first time we had been away from our families. We missed them terribly. Neither of us were drinkers, but we ended up drinking an entire bottle of whisky that night, reminiscing and re-living old memories. We would suffer for it the next day.

The last thing I remember, before we both dropped off to sleep, was David saying:

"But Charley, think of the adventure we have had…"

Spring finally arrived and we were able to go back to working our claim in earnest. I remember these as being good days in my life. David and I worked from sunup 'til sundown, most of the time. Long, exhausting days, but good days. The runoff from the melting snows gifted us with more gold and we harvested it gratefully. It was never the "big strike" that we were hoping for, but it was easily enough to keep us going. We played it down whenever we went into town or talked with other miners—we'd heard stories about miners who had made decent strikes and celebrated them, then somehow disappeared and were never heard from again.

By the beginning of August, our claim began to play out. We discussed staying for again for the winter, then decided that we both missed our families enormously and that we both wanted to go home. We had enough to go back for the winter, live fairly well, then return the following spring, and that was what we did.

One week before we left for New York, I was out working the claim alone. It was late morning and David had gone back to the cabin for something. I happened to look up and immediately stopped what I was doing. Fifty yards upstream from me and drinking from the river, was an enormous grizzly. Almost at the same moment, the bear looked up and saw me as well. Immediately, it stood up on its hind legs.

The beast was massive—easily eight feet tall and probably one-thousand pounds.

"Well, hello…bear," I heard myself say.

For a moment we stood, regarding each other. My rifle was within reach, but I didn't reach for it. Then David came walking up, rifle in hand. As soon as he saw the bear he stopped and whipped his rifle up to shoot. Without thinking I put my hands up, palms out, one hand at David and one at the bear.

"Hold on!" I said. "No one has to get hurt, here!"

David did not shoot. The bear stood for a moment longer, then dropped on to all fours. It bounced on its front paws once, chuffed and walked away from us.

Later, David would have a field day with this, telling everyone back home how I had put my hands up to stop both him and the bear (as if that would stop a bear from doing anything) and saying, "Hold on! No one has to get hurt, here!"

And somehow, that bear went from eight feet tall, to ten feet tall, in the telling. David also said he would have shot the bear anyway, despite my efforts, but it was so damn big he was afraid his bullet would just make it angry.

Our trip home and the subsequent trip back to California the following spring were, happily, without any incidents similar to what we had on our first trip. Both David and I were now considered "veterans of the trail". Folks looked to us for guidance. The two of us found that amusing. We were barely into our twenties, but people took us for old hands. We tried to be helpful where we could.

While in New York, our friends and families all commented on the change in David. In the past, he enjoyed the fact that people would cringe before his rapier wit. Now he was more subdued, almost kind. I knew he was still haunted by what the Pawnees had done to Otto Harrington, but I kept that to myself. The good and the bad adventures my cousin and I had shared over the past year had brought us closer. The effect of his words on that day had brought horror to David. I would not lay bare that horror for others to see. Let them think he had simply "matured". As indeed, he had.

Illinoistown received us back with open arms. This time, my older brother, Robert joined us. We were certain that this would be the year we hit it big. Unfortunately, that was not meant to be.

Fortunately for us, our cabin was still there and uninhabited. Our plan was to start there and take out what gold the river brought us during the winter, then to branch out and look for a better spot. That wasn't meant to be... We had barely settled in before, first Robert and then David became ill. Before a fortnight had passed, I buried them both.

Writing home of those two deaths is one of the hardest things I've ever had to do. I worked the claim alone that summer, although I seem to remember spending a lot of time, just sitting and staring off into space. What a lonely and terrible time that was! Still, by August, I had nearly as much as David and I had taken the previous year, and no one to share it with.

I had no wish to go home and face my family or friends, nor did I want to stay in the mountains for the winter. I considered spending the winter in San Francisco, then fortune smiled on me. One afternoon I was in Illinoistown, getting supplies, when I happened to see a familiar face. Walter Johnson was one year older than me. We had known each other back in Plassis, New York, where we had both grown up. Like me, he had turned to prospecting to make his fortune and, also like me, was grateful to encounter someone from home. We began to spend time together. His gold claim had played itself out, so I invited him to come out and spend the last few weeks working on my claim, out on the American River. After losing Robert and David and spending the entire summer alone, I can't tell you how good it felt to have company again. Walter had a quirky sense of humor that often left me in stitches from laughing. Like David and I had done a year earlier, he was heading east for the winter, not to New York, but to Decatur, Illinois. His uncle had moved there a year earlier with his family and he was planning to spend the winter with them. He invited me to join him. I supposed Illinois was as good as the next place, and I still had no wish to face my family and had no other plans, so I did just that. Looking back, I think Walter had it in his head all along, that I should marry his cousin…

Mary Elizabeth Johnson had been a little girl the last time I had seen her, back in New York. When I met her again in Decatur she was fifteen, eight years younger than I was. I found her to be bright and attractive—and frustrating. From the day we met she seemed to take issue with anything and everything I said. Her cousin Walter' and I shared a flat together, and on Sundays the two of us were always invited over for dinner. After a while I stopped going due to the constant confrontations with Mary. When Walter asked me about it I told him it was due to Mary's arguing with me any time that I voiced an opinion of any kind.

"You really don't understand women much, do you Charley?"

"Well, I like to think I do…why?"

"She's just trying to get a reaction from you! Any reaction! She's doing it because she actually *likes* you!"

That gave me something to think about. The following Sunday I once more joined the Johnson clan for dinner. Mary seemed subdued and aloof that day. I even attempted to draw her into an argument, but she ignored me. I was nearly convinced that Walter had been wrong, yet before I left that day I asked her: "There is new play downtown—*The Corsican Brothers*—* would you care to go and see it with me? Assuming that it is all right with your father…"

She responded with some of the fire that I had become accustomed to.

"I assure you, Mr. Boles, that it will be just fine with father!" Then, "Yes—I would love to see a play."

The following Friday we went to dinner first, then went on to the play, escorted by

Mary's entire family. Nevertheless, the two of us were there "together". After that we began to spend more and more time together. By the time spring once more rolled around, we were in love.

—"The Corsican Brothers"*, by Alexandre Dumas, 1848

Walter and I again headed for the gold fields. I wrote to Mary nearly every day, and she in turn, wrote to me. Her letters brought me a sort of excruciating joy, and I read them over and over again. When we returned to Decatur that fall, I asked for her hand in marriage, and she said yes.

Our engagement lasted through the winter. It had been in my mind that we should marry in Decatur, but Mary absolutely would not hear of it. Both of us had family and friends back in

New York, and if she was going to marry me, it would have to be there. I dreaded seeing my family again, had even changed the spelling of my name from "Bowles" to "Boles" from some misguided sense of guilt over losing Robert and David to illness. Our reunion was agonizing and tearful and, in the end, the best thing that could have happened. My sense of guilt over not being able to save my beloved brother and cousin were enormous. My family held no such incriminations. My older brother, William, chided me: "You fool, Charley—don't you understand that, by staying away, you made us feel that we had lost three family members, not just two…"

The lessoning of my sense of guilt made the wedding a much happier event than I could have hoped for. It took place in early June, 1854. After a short honeymoon touring New England, Mary and I returned to Decatur as man and wife.

Those early years with Mary were a happy, happy time. I once more accepted a job working in a sawmill. I still had money saved from the gold I had found and we planned to use that to buy a farm, near Decatur. A letter from Walter changed that plan. He had met a young woman in New Oregon, in Howard County, Iowa, and said it was the "perfect place" to live. Mary and I packed our things and moved there. Our first daughter, Ida Martha, was born on our farm there in April of 1857. A year later we sold that farm and, for a time, returned and lived in Jefferson County, New York, where we both still had family and friends. Our second daughter, Eva Ardella, was born there. We then returned to Decatur, where our third daughter, Frances Lillian, was born in June of 1861.

By this time the nation had erupted in civil war. Mary begged me not to go and, for a time, I agreed. Everyone thought it would all be over in six months, and I needed to provide for my family. We were all wrong. The war dragged on and on. In the end, I felt compelled to go and serve. On August 13, 1862, I signed a three-year enlistment with the 116th Infantry Regiment, out of Macon County, Illinois, and prepared to fight for The Union Army.

I ended up in Company B, 2nd squad, which was mostly made up of men and boys from Decatur. Our squad leader was a young school teacher named Christian Reibsame. Christian was a quiet man with brown hair and blue eyes.

He was immediately likeable, stood ramrod straight, and had a confidence about himself that made you trust him. He never cursed, was never disparaging and would not allow himself to get discouraged. To me he seemed the perfect choice for squad leader.

The other men in my squad were Abe Shepherd, Rueben Bills, Sam Bradshaw, Tom Burgess, Jim Sherman, George Patterson, Patrick Noland and Mike Kelly. Shepherd was dark and serious. Rueben Bills had light brown hair and blue eyes and spoke often of his wife, Betsy and his son, William. Sam Bradshaw was an attorney from Newburg. He had red hair and brown eyes and reminded me of my late cousin, David, because he had the same wit and humor that David had. Tom Burgess was a nervous, mousy little fellow that the rest of us tended to avoid. George Patterson and I quickly became best friends. He was taller than me, with dark hair and eyes. He had a devil-may-care attitude and was, according to the ladies, devilishly handsome. Patrick Noland and Mike Kelly were regular chaps. Kelly had auburn hair and green eyes; Noland had dark hair and eyes.

And then there was me—light hair, blue eyes. I missed my wife and daughters as much as Rueben missed his family, I'm certain, but I tried not to burden the others with it.

For nearly three months, we stayed and trained in Decatur, which meant that I was able to see my family on a regular basis. I invited

George to come and stay with us on several of those occasions. Mary thought he was the cat's meow.

On November 8th, 1862, we left Decatur and headed for the fighting.

FIVE

BY THE end of November, we were in Memphis, Tennessee. We joined Major General Sherman's Fifteenth Army Corps and were assigned to the First Brigade, Second Division. Under Sherman's command we headed out again, this time heading for the Tallahatchie River. On December 13th we arrived, only to turn around and head back to Memphis. From there we began marching down the Mississippi to the Yazoo River, which we followed for fifteen miles before reaching Chickasaw Bayou. This was where we would see our first action. For weaponry I carried a Springfield 1855 musket (which was capable of firing both musket balls and the new Minnie ball) a Remington 1858 revolver, a sixteen-inch Bowie knife, and the Cree tomahawk that my cousin David had given me eleven years earlier. I felt pretty formidable, but then, it's easy to feel formidable until the other side starts shooting. And those southern boys could shoot.

Taking the town of Vicksburg, Mississippi was an important goal for the Union Army, for a number of reasons. Doing so would split the Confederate forces and would give

Union Army access to the sea, but taking it would not prove easy.

On December 26th, 1862 we were ordered to push the Confederates back so that the rest of General Sherman's army could attack their flank, and at first we were successful. We ran a running battle over Mrs. Lake's Plantation, pushing the rebs back to Chickasaw Bluffs, but that was about as far as we got. They had fortifications set up that they were able to put into place as they retreated—and which slowed us. The first of these was a line of abatis—sharpened rods that were tied to logs, forming a horizontal tripod with the spikes aimed at us. These were tied together, forming a line that was all but impossible to get through while you were under fire. After this we had to cross Chickasaw Bayou, a chest-deep patch of murky water that had to be traversed, with the rebel army firing on us from the bluffs above.

That battle lasted three days and ended with the Union Army withdrawing in defeat. We sustained casualties numbering nearly 1,800. Later we heard that the south lost less than 200. Although we lost, the 116th showed valor in battle. We received high compliments from the seasoned veterans that we fought beside.

It was my first time to see men fall in battle. It would, by far, not be my last.

Nor would I have long to wait for our next engagement. After losing the day at Chickasaw

Bayou, Sherman began moving us back up the Mississippi, where we encountered Major General John McClurnand. Although they were both Major Generals, McClurnand outranked Sherman and ordered us to join forces with him. Then, ignoring his orders to attack Vicksburg, McClurnand turned us up the Arkansas River, where we attacked Fort Lindeman at Arkansas Post on January 11th, 1863.

Arriving too late to go into battle the night before, on January 10th, we set up camp and waited.

Between McClernand's and Sherman's forces, we had about 30,000 men. We were also joined by a flotilla of gunboats and ironclads, led by Admiral Porter. It was the first time I'd seen ironclad ships. They were something to behold.

The following morning we set up and then waited for orders to attack. Waiting is always the hardest time. Everyone has the jitters—some more than others—and fear is contagious.

Don't ever let anyone tell you different. Our unit commander, First Lieutenant John Taylor, remained composed throughout the morning and did his best to bolster the men. His actions and words helped. Watching him, I couldn't help but be reminded of what Captain Hallowell had told me, years earlier, when we were crossing the plains:

"Fear isn't real. It seems real, but it isn't. It's a reaction to a certain situation. If you can remember that when things get tight, it'll help you keep control, and maybe save your life."

Fear certainly felt like a real thing that day, I can tell you. I relayed his words to those around me. Some of them shared it with others, who passed the story on to Lieutenant Taylor, who then commended me for it and used Hallowell's words to inspire the rest of the unit. In spite of that, when the noon meal came, many were too sick with fear to eat. Others, who did manage to choke their food down, ended up vomiting it up afterward.

It seemed that we had just finished our meal when we were finally ordered to attack.

The Navy began first. At mid-morning they had begun to bombard Fort Hindeman and the surrounding fortifications. The rebels had built the fort up from what it had been before. It was made almost in the shape of a square star. The walls were 300 feet wide and indented at the middle, which allowed shooters at each end of the wall to fire down upon attackers and catch them in a crossfire. They also had rifle pits dug around the fort, full of riflemen. Just getting to the fort was a challenge in itself. It was surrounded by a dry moat, twenty feet wide and eight feet deep. This had to be crossed and we were under fire the entire time.

The Navy guns had done their work, both on the parapet and on the rifle pits, but those rebel boys still had plenty of fight in them. Abe Shepherd was just ahead of me. He went down and I almost tripped over him. Then the man on my left took a bullet to the chest and fell. I kept going and made it to what little protection the far side of the moat offered. There were several of us gathered there. We took a moment to catch our breath, then went up and over the embankment. Men on either side of me took lead and collapsed, but somehow I was untouched. I ran toward one of the rifle pits, firing my rifle at the two men stationed there. One of them fell. The other man aimed his rifle at me and squeezed the trigger.

I think my brother, Robert, was looking out for me that day, or maybe my cousin David. I should have been dead then and there, but the rifle misfired. Then I was in the pit with him and we were fighting hand to hand. I attempted a butt-stroke with my rifle, the rebel parried it and tried to bayonet me. I managed to knock it away, striking his left hand in the process and causing him to drop his rifle. Quickly, I moved in and bayoneted him in the chest.

Everything after that was a blur. I remember attacking one man with my knife and my tomahawk. He fired a pistol at me, hitting the tomahawk instead. The tomahawk flew away and I attacked him with my Bowie knife. Sometime after that, everything just stopped.

White flags were flying all along the parapet. The rebels were surrendering.

We had won the day, but again had taken heavy losses. A number of men from Company B were killed, and among them were Privates Abe Shepherd and Rueben Bills, and Lieutenant Taylor.

I tried looking for what might be left of my tomahawk, but never found it. What was more upsetting to me was the fact that we were barely into this war, and already two members of my squad were gone.

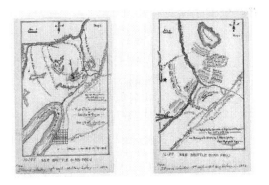

*Maps of Chickasaw Bayou by Munn, E. A. (Edward A.) 1892 (—Civil War Maps created by the Army Corps of Engineers)

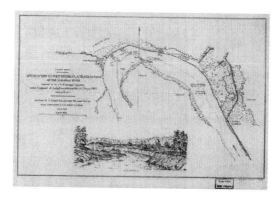

*Arkansas Post 1863 (—Civil War Maps created by the Army Corps of Engineers)

SIX

WE STAYED at Fort Hindeman for several days. On January 19th, we lost another member of our squad. Tom Burgess failed to show up at muster and was listed as a deserter.

Toward the end of January, we were ordered to move to Young's Point, along the Mississippi River, where we stayed for nearly two months. That proved to be a bad time for the 116th. Many of the men took sick and died from dysentery, ague, or swamp fever. Truth was, we lost more men there to illness than we had in two battles. Tom Bradshaw, who reminded me of my late cousin, David, was one of those. He came down with swamp fever and died on April 3rd, 1863. Our squad was now down by three. Other men replaced them, but I could not tell you their names.

Actually, the squad was down by four at that point. On January 8th, Christian Reibsame was promoted to First Lieutenant and left our squad, and I became squad leader.

On March 18th, we boarded the steamship *Silver Wave*, which took us up the Mississippi to Black Bayou. There, we met up once more with

General Sherman. It took all day to transport all of the troops that were scheduled to meet there and by the time we formed up, it was dark. General Sherman himself led us by candle light through a canebrake for roughly two miles. We set up camp in the dark at Hill's plantation. The next morning, we received our orders. Admiral Porter had taken four ironclads up Deer Creek in an effort to find a back way to the Yazoo River. If successful, it would allow our troops to move around the rebel army and attack from their left flank. Deer Creek apparently had a lot of obstructions, which had slowed Porter to a crawl. We were to go up and clear the obstructions, allowing him to get through.

We had traveled only a short distance, when General Sherman was met by a runner. A rebel force had blocked Porter's way by falling trees into Deer Creek ahead of him. The force, roughly 400 men, had then moved downstream from Porter and his ironclads and were falling trees there, preventing Porter's retreat and trapping the ironclads. General Sherman ordered us to proceed with all haste to go to Porter's aid. He would wait for the next regiment to be brought up by boat, and then would join us.

It was twenty-one miles up Deer Creek to Admiral Porter's location. We alternately ran and fast-walked. The rebels had dropped trees into the creek both ahead and behind the ironclads, trapping them where they were. Porter's men were trapped inside the boats, as every time a man would try to go out on deck, sharpshooters would pick them off from the trees lining the creek. We joined the fight as soon as we arrived, and a bitter battle ensued that lasted until General Sherman arrived with more men. Then the rebels were routed.

We spent the next few days clearing Deer creek of debris, which allowed Admiral Porter's ironclads to back down out of Deer Creek and back to the main waterway.

The plan to find an alternate route to the Yazoo River was cancelled after that. General Grant gave up his plan for striking the rebel army's left flank, and instead concentrated on attacking on the right.

Sometime later, we learned that those ironclads we helped save were worth more than $3,000,000.00 which, at that time, was almost more money than I could conceive of.

In May, the final push for Vicksburg began, and we saw some of the bloodiest fighting yet. On May 16th, we were ordered to take Champion's Hill. The rebs were dug in on the bluffs overlooking a three-mile stretch of Jackson Creek, and we were ordered to take it away from them. We were lined up along Jackson Road and for us, it was all uphill. Around 11:30 we gave a mighty yell and began running up the hill, lead flying everywhere. We pushed and they gave ground. Then they pushed back and we gave ground. The fighting was bitter and intense. Around me men screamed and died. Gun smoke was so thick in the air it made it hard to see the enemy. We fought back and forth, giving ground then taking it again. Around 1:00 PM our superior numbers prevailed and we finally took Champion's Hill. Then the rebs rallied with fresh troops and took it back from us, but they weren't able to take as much as they'd had at the beginning.

Then General Grant ordered in fresh troops and we charged once more. This time we won the day. The rebels gave up Champion's Hill once and for all and withdrew to the Black River Bridge, where we engaged them the following day. Once more the fighting was intense. My company took heavy losses on those days, and on the days that followed. Many good men and good officers died. I began to wonder if any of us were going to make it through this war, but I was careful to keep those thoughts to myself.

The rebs fought just as hard at Black River Bridge as they did at Champion Hill. In the end, we forced them back across the river. They burned the bridge so that we couldn't use it to follow them. This forced General Pemburton's confederate forces to withdraw into the fortress city of Vicksburg, and it would only be a matter of time before we took that.

The next two days saw two major assaults against the town of Vicksburg, but we weren't able to break through and again, took heavy casualties. On May 25th, General Grant ordered us to pull back and rest. That proved to be one day too late for another member of my squad, Jim Sherman. Jim had been a quiet, likeable chap. A bit of a dreamer, he'd kept a diary and often spoke of becoming a writer when the war was over. On May 24th, he took a bullet to the chest. He died the following day.

We couldn't get in, but the rebels could not get out, and we knew their supplies were low. It would be only a matter of time before they either surrendered, or died of starvation. This gave us a chance to lick our wounds and re-supply.

Pemburton's forces stubbornly held out for more than a month. By then they were out of food and starving.

On July 1,1863 I received a promotion to First Sergeant. I wasn't sure if this was a blessing or a curse, but it meant more money for Mary and the girls, so I suppose it was a good thing. Three days later, their supplies gone and their spirits shattered, the rebs finally surrendered, and we took Vicksburg.

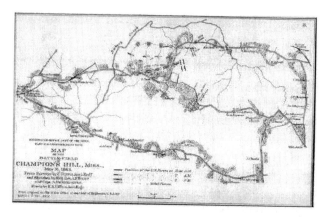

*Champion's Hill (—Civil War Maps created by the Army Corps of Engineers)

*Vicksburg Map by Robert Knox Sneden, 1863 (—Civil War Maps created by the Army Corps of Engineers)

SEVEN

WE ENGAGED in one more exercise that summer, which began on July 5th, but had to do no real fighting. We pursued General Johnston and his command, who withdrew ahead of us, past Jackson to the Pearl River. Then we were ordered back to camp Sherman, where we enjoyed a season of rest. By now we were all aged veterans. We knew that this war was far from over and that we would be needed and would have to fight again. We also knew that Vicksburg was a major victory for us. The tide of the war had turned in our favor. At the same time that the rebs were surrendering to us at Vicksburg, another major battle had been won in the north, at Gettysburg, Pennsylvania. It was now a matter of time before the Union would win, but the rebs were determined not to give up. There would be many casualties on both sides before the fighting was done. Unfortunately, I would be one of them.

In October we headed out again, marching first to Memphis, then on to Chattanooga. We arrived on November 21st, and two nights later, on pontoon boats, we floated down the Tennessee River to the mouth of

Chickamauga Creek. Under the command of General Giles A. Smith, we captured all the rebel pickets and were able to hold the position until the entire Corps passed through and got set up. The next day we advanced to the base of Lookout Mountain, where we engaged the rebels in a lively skirmish throughout the day. By evening we had captured Lookout Mountain, but it wasn't without losses. During that engagement General Smith was gravely wounded. Although he would survive until after the war was over, the wounds he received that day would eventually kill him.

The following morning, on November 25th, we crossed the river and attacked Missionary Ridge. After General Smith was injured, Colonel N.W. Tupper took command of the 116th. Colonel Tupper was a man that every soldier in the unit looked up to and thought of as a friend. He was the type of leader that every officer aspires to be, the kind of commander that men would follow anywhere.

After taking Lookout Mountain, we took our position on the far left flank of General Sherman's Army. Most of the fighting was done at the center of the lines that day and for once, we saw little action. At the end of the day, Chattanooga was ours.

*Chattanooga (—Civil War Maps created by the Army Corps of Engineers)

*The Battle of Missionary Ridge (—Civil War
Maps created by the Army Corps of Engineers)

We had left our coats and blankets back
in camp, on the other side of the river. Instead of
letting us return and retrieve our supplies, we
were ordered to force-march our way to
Knoxville to help relieve General Burnside.
Burnside had taken Knoxville a few months
earlier, but now was in danger of losing it back to
Longstreet's confederate army. General Grant
wanted us there as quickly as possible, to make

sure that didn't happen. By day, we marched 25 – 30 miles, and the activity kept us warm enough, but the nights were pure misery. With no coats or blankets to keep us warm, we built huge bonfires and huddled around them. The bonfires kept us alive, but only barely.

December of 1863 is a month I will never forget. Besides almost freezing, food supplies were low and we nearly starved as well. At one point we had only hardtack to eat—a dry, hard cracker that some of the boys referred to as "molar breakers". Later, I would learn that those rebels boys ate cornbread. Hardtack wasn't so bad, if you dipped it into your coffee—but it wasn't cornbread.

Our being in Knoxville did what it intended, however. With Burnside reinforced with fresh recruits (that being us) Longstreet decided not to attack.

It was mid-January before we finally left Knoxville for our winter quarters in Larkinsville, Alabama. We stayed there until the beginning of May, when we were dispatched to fight once more. It was during this time that I received another promotion, this time to Second Lieutenant. This was not a commission that I wanted, but again, I accepted it. Also, during this time, Colonel Tupper took ill and died. That hit us all hard. I felt as though I had lost a personal friend, and knew the others did as well.

*Battle of Resaca, Georgia (—Civil War Maps created by the Army Corps of Engineers

On May 14, we were in Resaca, Georgia. Resaca lies along the north bank of the Oostanaula River. It is a place of quicksand and steep, muddy banks. This was a day when I learned just how little I liked being an officer. Going into battle when you have only your own skin to take care of is one thing, but going in when you are responsible for a hundred others is something else entirely. We were hotly engaged that day, and on the following day. The men fought valiantly, but we still took heavy losses. I felt responsible for each of them.

Following the battle of Resaca I received yet another promotion, this time to First Lieutenant. Again I accepted the appointment with reluctance. It was a rank that would I hold for but a short time.

The rebels retreated from Resaca and we followed. On May 25 we caught them at New Hope Church and it was a disaster. General Sherman, believing the rebel force to be minimal, ordered General Hooker to attack. The rebs were dug in and waiting. Hooker's men were slaughtered by the hundreds and driven back. The next day, May 26th, began with artillery fire. I remember little of that day for, somewhere during it all, a bullet struck me down low and on my right side, and all I knew was nausea and pain.

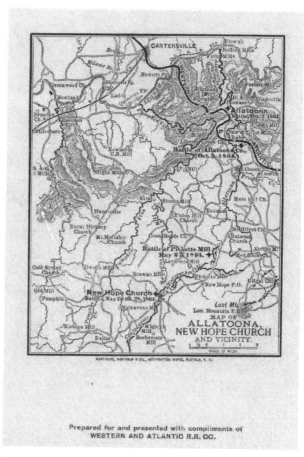

*The Battle of New Hope Church, where Charley was wounded (—Civil War Maps created by the Army Corps Of Engineers)

EIGHT

I AWOKE in agony, in an Army hospital, where I would spend the next six weeks. I had been shot in the lower part of my abdomen. Gut shot. By their whispers, I could tell that the doctors and nurses in attendance did not expect me to live. I can tell you there were times, in those first couple of weeks, when I wished they had been right. Such misery as that seems almost beyond human endurance. I had heard that being gut shot was one of the worst ways to go, and I'm here to bear testament that, for my money, that statement is true. I couldn't tell you how many times, in those first days, that I woke up, only to pass out again because the pain was too great to bear. Slowly, though, I began to mend. During my fourth week there Major Nolan, the chief surgeon at the hospital, came by to check my progress. After going over my chart, he checked the wound, then said, "Well, congratulations, Sergeant, it looks as though you're going to live."

"Sergeant? Sir, you must have the wrong chart. My rank is First Lieutenant."

"Not any longer. They've demoted you back to First Sergeant. Not for any wrongdoing, mind you. Everyone thought you were going to die, and a widow's pension for a sergeant is less than that of an officer. Trust the Army to always do what is best for the Army. Don't worry though, there's plenty of war left. You'll have plenty of time to get promoted again before the fighting stops."

My disappointment at being demoted was slight, my relief great. If they had demoted me back to Private I would have been just as glad. Bearing responsibility for other men is not anything I ever aspired to. And wearing the guilt that comes with watching them die in agony takes a strength I never wanted to have.

It is also distracting. When you are looking out for others, and inspiring them to run out and get killed, you have less time to look out after yourself. Having now been an officer, I had much more respect for the good officers we had in the regiment, but I had absolutely no desire to rejoin their ranks.

Over the years, I've tried to recall the events of that day, May 26th, 1864, but my mind shuts it out. Probably just as well.

During the fifth week of my stay in the hospital I received the unhappy news that my good friend George Patterson had been killed at the battle of Kennesaw Mountain. That news hit me hard. George had been such a bright light! I found it unfathomable that he could be gone.

Of my original squad, only me, Noland, Kelly and Christian Reibsame—now *Captain* Reibsame—remained. And the war was not yet over.

Toward the end of July I was finally released from the hospital and ordered to check back once a week until further notice, to have my wound inspected. I was ordered "light duty", but at first even that was too much for me. It was hard to believe how weak I had become or how doing almost nothing exhausted me. It would be weeks before I would find myself declared fit for active duty and to return to the 116th. And many more weeks before I would feel like myself again.

If you have a choice, I would advise never being wounded in the abdomen.

In late August I finally received orders to rejoin my unit—just before the battle at Jonesborough, Georgia. Although I had been cleared for active duty at the hospital, the company doctor ordered that I wait out the coming battle. I did so with mixed emotions. I had improved greatly in the previous weeks, but was still nowhere near my full strength and vitality. Battle is exhausting. Part of me was glad to stay out of the fight, but another part of me wanted to be with my unit and I felt guilty for not being there. I had been nearly mortally wounded, yet I was anxious to get back in the thick of it. This came from a feeling of resignation that I was either going to make it through this war or not. Either way, I wanted to get it over with. Everyone knew, after the battles of Vicksburg and Gettysburg, that the South was beaten—except for the South. We had cut their supply lines and forced them back, but they stubbornly refused to accept defeat. Many good men on both sides would die because of that stubbornness. If I was to be one of them I would rather it happened sooner than later. No one wants to be the last casualty in a war.

And before that day came, if it came, I was determined to make those rebel boys pay for it. Heavily.

Nor did I have long to wait. On September 2nd, we marched into Atlanta. Confederate General Hood had vacated the town ahead of us, only the day before. We did not destroy the town but took it. We also took food supplies and livestock, and at General Sherman's command, forced the locals to leave the city. We received word that General Hood denounced Sherman's barbarity, to which Sherman replied, "War is Cruelty. You cannot refine it. You may as well appeal against the thunder storm as against these terrible hardships of war." He wanted the rebs—the soldiers and the civilians alike, to know they were beaten and their cause was lost. Some have said his methods were heavy-handed, but it accomplished what he wanted them to.

In November, General Sherman began what would become known as his "March To The Sea", or "The Savanah Campaign". We arrived just outside of Savanah on December 12. The following morning we were one of nine regiments ordered to storm the fort. The bugle sounded and we charged. A few shots were fired. A few men and officers were killed or wounded, but less than ten minutes after the charge began, our colors were flying over the parapet.

Savanah by the sea is a beautiful town. We stayed there for a few days, then again continued on with the war.

"The Carolinas Campaign" was, mostly, a mopping up operation. We chased the Confederates and they withdrew ahead of us. General Sherman made it clear that, while we were to treat local civilians with no particular kindness, there was to be no raping or unnecessary killing. He wanted to take the fight out of the southerners, but not completely destroy them. When we entered South Carolina, which happened to be the first state to secede from the union, some of the men grew bitter. On February 17th, we entered the capitol city of Columbia. Despite orders to the contrary, the town was burned to the ground.

We were headed north, headed home. Every man of us knew it, though we rarely mentioned it. On March 19th thru 21st, we engaged the enemy for our last time, at Bentonville, North Carolina. Once again, we won the day after a three-day fight. After that, it was all downhill for us. The following month, on April 9th, General Lee surrendered at Appomattox, Virginia, and the war was officially over.

But then it wasn't. The celebratory feeling that we all felt was short-lived. April 14th was Good Friday. We were all happy that the war was over and looking forward to celebrating a happy, peaceful Easter. That feeling ended around ten o'clock that night, when we were once more put on high alert. Earlier that evening, President Lincoln had been watching a play, *My American Cousin*, when an actor named John Wilkes Booth crept into the Presidential box and shot him in the back of his head. The following morning, and for the next 29 days, all American flags flew at half-mast.

We in the military stayed on high alert. No one knew what to expect. Lee had surrendered, but there were still southern generals that hadn't given up. For the weeks that followed we waited. Andrew Johnson became our new president. None of us knew if we would be called again to fight or not.

On April 26th, members of the 16th New York Cavalry trapped John Wilkes Booth and another man, David E. Harold inside a barn at Garrett's farm, near Port Royal, Virginia. The two men refused to come out, so the Army set the barn on fire. Harold left the barn and was captured, but Booth remained inside. Then a soldier (who later claimed Booth was aiming a rifle at him) shot Booth in the neck. Booth was brought out of the barn. Apparently, his last words were, "Useless, useless..." To me, a better word would have been "senseless..."

That same day, Confederate General Joseph E. Johnston surrendered with 30,000 of his men. We all breathed a sigh of relief. There were still a few guerilla groups fighting, but the war, finally, was truly over.

On June 7, 1865, I mustered out of the Army with the rank of First Sergeant, near Washington D.C., and headed for home. The other three remaining members of my original squad mustered out with me. Noland, Kelly and I were standing together, when Captain Christian Reibsame walked over to us. I started to salute, then nodded.

"Captain," I said.

"Not captain anymore, Charley. I'm a civilian now, just like you." Then, "Gentlemen, congratulations! We made it!"

I grunted. "Four out of ten," I said. "Wish the others could be here..."

"As do we all, Charley," Reibsame said. "But at least *we* are here."

They say that two kinds of men came out of that war. Tens of thousands of men, having become inured to the cruelties of battle, continued on with lives of violence and bloodshed and created far more brutal ugliness in the west than any fiction could ever portray. I was the second type. Having seen enough death and destruction to last two lifetimes, I hoped I would never have to encounter it again.

NINE

DURING THE war, Mary had taken the girls and gone to live with her brother in New Oregon, Iowa. I joined them there. The joy I felt at seeing my wife and my girls again is almost impossible to describe. For days I would wake up, not quite believing that I was really back with my family. We bought a small farm and began to build our life again.

Peace. It is just a word, until it gets taken from you. If you're lucky enough to get it back it becomes something that you cherish. It didn't matter that I'd been shot, the pain and the cold, the starving and hell that I'd seen and been through. I was home and with my family, and I never wanted to leave them again.

It was the middle of August. I'd spent the day in the fields, tending the corn and wishing that I was the farmer my father had been. I stopped at the pump and filled a bucket with water, then walked on up to the house, stopping on the porch to wash up before going inside.

Supper was nearly ready. Mary seemed strangely quiet. I watched her for a few minutes, waiting. Finally she turned to me and said, simply, "I'm pregnant again, Charley. We're going to have another child."

I watched her for a moment, unsure if she was happy or sad. Then I went to her and took her in my arms.

"Mary, that's wonderful! Are you certain?"

"Yes, I am. It's about two months, I think." Then, "It means another mouth to feed…"

"We'll manage," I told her, feeling an uncomfortable twinge. "We'll be fine!"

"I know, Charley. I know we will."

That was the first time I began to wonder about my role as a provider for my family. Mary and I had made the decision to buy the farm together. It had seemed an easy decision at the time. We had both grown up on farms. Other than that, I had experience working in a sawmill, as a gold miner and as a soldier. Farming had seemed the obvious choice.

In April of 1866 my son, Arian, was born. That was one of the happiest events of my life. I loved my girls dearly. After coming home from the war mostly intact, being blessed with a son was more than I could ask for.

Those were happy times. I would work through the day and come in at night, eager to see my family and make sure they were all right, and

I looked forward to a bountiful harvest that would allow me to give my family the things they both needed and deserved.

On our farm we grew a little bit of everything, but our cash crops were wheat and corn. If things went well at harvest, we would have enough to make it through the winter and make it easily through to the following year. In July everything looked great, but in mid August I began to notice some wilting in both crops. It wasn't long before I knew what the problem was—cinch bugs. Cinch bugs are a parasite that attacks both corn and wheat. They are a foul-smelling little pest, especially when crushed, and they ruin your crops. I tried pulling up the infected plants and burning them, but in the end I lost nearly three-quarters of my corn and my wheat. Later, I heard that many farms in our neighboring Kansas were completely wiped out by the parasite, so I guess we were lucky. But it didn't feel like it at the time.

The happiness I had known in early summer gave way to a miserable winter. We were nearly destitute, better off than some families who had been affected by the blight, but broke to the point that I wondered how we could make it through to spring. Christmas was dismal. Mary made clothes for the girls and the baby, and a shirt for me. I managed to scrape together enough to buy her a small locket for her. It was nowhere near the comfortable time that I had been hoping for. The guilt I felt for it was enormous.

As spring approached I began to hear stories of other farmers who were planning to plant their farms with cranberries, which were apparently resistant to cinch bugs. When I brought that up to Mary, she surprised me.

"Charley," she began, "when we first got married you were a gold miner. You were happy-go-lucky and always had plenty of money. You're not a farmer—you are a lot of things, but that isn't one of them. I know you feel you have to stay here and take care of us, but I think you would do better to go and find us some gold and maybe make us all rich. The girls and I can take care of the farm…"

I looked at her for a moment.

"You've given this some thought," I told her.

"Yes. Yes I have. I've given it a lot of thought. You aren't happy and I know you feel guilty about losing the crops, but that was God's work. You did all you could and you managed to save at least some of it. That's better than what others ended up with! Go and find us some gold. Let me and the girls manage here. If you send us some money occasionally, we'll be better off. You were good at finding gold! Go and make us rich!"

I didn't know whether to feel dejected or relieved by her words, so I felt a little of both. I could think of nothing to say to her. For a moment we just stood there. Then she started to turn away. I reached out and pulled her to me.

"If you honestly feel that would be best, I'll do it," I told her.

"I honestly do," she said.

And two weeks later, I headed back to the gold fields.

This time, rather than go all the way to California, I decided to try my luck in Montana. We said our tearful goodbyes and I hugged my family and then left them. At first I felt guilty for leaving them again, especially Arian, but as the road opened before me I realized that Mary was right. Seeing her every day, and carrying guilt for losing our crops had left me feeling lost, like a failure. Now I was free again. Still attached, but free. I could do better for us out in the gold fields, but I never would have left if she hadn't suggested it. I'm sure she knew that, too.

In almost no time I had established a claim on Deer Creek, outside of Silver Bow, Montana. I had a partner, Henry Roberts, from Missouri. Henry was a quiet man who spoke little but worked hard. We were working "Long Toms", which were a kind of sluice box. I spent my days shoveling sand from the creek into it, and letting the flow of water from the creek wash the sand away. Small nuggets and gravel would collect in the box, from where I would fetch them. The trick to making this work is understanding the path that gold, which is heavier than the other material in the creek, takes when it washes down a river or a creek. If you knew that you could sometimes do all right.

We didn't make a fortune from this, but every day we found gold.

I sent money to Mary and the kids that month, and on following months. When the winter snows arrived I left Henry and headed back to the farm. I told him I would return early in the spring, when we would once more resume our hunt for gold.

That winter was as good as the previous one had been awful. The farm had made some money, but with what I was able to bring home from the gold fields we were in good shape. Mary and I went overboard buying gifts at Christmas, trying to make up to the girls for what had been lacking the year before. I stayed long enough to celebrate Arian's second birthday, then headed back to Deer Creek.

The next couple of years went on like that, Mary and the girls working the farm and me out hunting gold in the summertime and home for winter. Each time I came home I was amazed at how much bigger Arian had gotten. He was a happy and inquisitive boy. He brightened my days. The girls, meanwhile, were turning into beautiful young women. Each time I left it seemed harder than the time before. I missed my family terribly, especially my son.

While I was gone Henry would work the claim when the weather permitted. Whatever he found he kept for himself, as per our agreement. He didn't go overboard on this—some miners worked their claim no matter how harsh the weather was. Many lost fingers and toes to frostbite. Henry, mostly, played at it and kept an eye on things.

We had made friends with our neighbors, for there are times when miners need to stick together even though they're in competition with each other. One afternoon, while working our claim, we heard gunshots. Grabbing our rifles, we set out at a run. A short while later we were on a low hill overlooking a claim operated by the Sweeney brothers, Kevin and Kim. The two men were under attack by a party of four Blackfoot Indians, who had them pinned down.

Checking to make sure that my cover was secure, I opened fire on the Indians. I intentionally missed my first shot, throwing dirt into the face of the Indian nearest me. I wanted to get the Indian's attention and let them know the Sweeney's weren't alone, but I didn't necessarily want to kill them. Henry followed my lead.

The ruse worked. In a matter of moments the Indians were on their ponies and riding away.

Kevin Sweeney had a hole in his pantleg and a bullet-burn on his leg, but other than that, the two men were unhurt.

"Lucky I looked up and saw them when I did," Kevin told me. "Otherwise, they would have caught us both out in the open and we'd probably be dead, now. Good thing you men showed up when you did! Thanks!"

"You're welcome," I said. "Do you think they'll come back?"

"Probably not, but you never can tell with Indians. There have been more and more isolated attacks by the Sioux, the Cheyenne or the Blackfeet. The 7th Cavalry is here to keep them in check, but they can't be everywhere. Those three tribes hate us. Any man caught alone is done for. Keep a sharp eye—if we hear you shooting, we'll be along to return the favor."

We went back to our claim, fully aware that it was only luck that the Indians had stumbled onto the Sweeney's first, and not us. I spent the rest of the afternoon looking over my shoulder and getting little work done.

One day I went into town for supplies. There was a letter from Mary. I immediately opened it and read:

My Dearest Charley,

It is with the heaviest of hearts that I have to tell you of the death of our son, Arian. Last week, we were working the fields and he was off to one side, playing, when I noticed that his little cheeks were flushed. I felt his forehead and he was quite warm, so I immediately took him home and put him to bed. I sent Eve into town to fetch the Doctor, who gave Arian medicines. It was to no avail. Arian is gone, Charley. Our little boy is forever gone.

I struggle to be strong, to keep things together for the girls, but I am broken inside. My heart is broken and I know that now, yours is too. I am so, so sorry.

Your Loving Wife,

Mary

I read the letter in disbelief, then read it again, tears falling onto the page. It couldn't be true. It couldn't!

"No," I heard myself say. "No. No. No. No. No...!" My voice cracked and became plaintive. Then my chest heaved and I buried my face in my hands and wept uncontrollably. People on the street looked at me, but I couldn't stop myself, nor did I care.

I don't remember returning to the cabin that day. The weeks that followed are a dull, hazy, painful memory. I felt as if I'd been gutshot again. I could have found all the gold in Montana and it would not have mattered.

I eventually wrote back to Mary, telling her how sorry I was and that I knew she had done everything possible to save our son. Part of me wanted to blame her. Deep down, I knew it was God's will. Mary could have called every doctor in Iowa, but it wouldn't have stopped God from taking my boy away from me.

To this day, I still tear up when I remember reading that letter, the day I learned of the death of my little boy.

When I returned home that winter Mary and the girls met me and we all wept. This time it wasn't tears of joy, but of grief. It was a sad, strained season for all of us, during which Mary and I seemed to grow apart. When I returned to Montana in the spring I felt relieved at my going, and I believe Mary did too.

TEN

BECAUSE OF THE Indian unrest, I considered moving on out to California. Our claim was producing steadily, so we stayed. My trips into town became more frequent, but there we had to be careful, too. People noticed how often you showed up, what you spent and how you paid. A lone miner was an easy target for whites as well as Indians. Our claim never did give us a big payday, but it gave us enough to keep us there and keep us hoping. I learned to work with a six-gun strapped to my waist and my rifle within easy reach. And to sleep with one eye open. The end of the Civil War had turned thousands of men into the west, many willing to kill without hesitation to get what they wanted. Diligence was the price of staying alive.

First I saw the dust, then I saw the riders—two white men. I kept working until they were within one-hundred yards, then I stopped and waited for them. Both wore pistols, but they had a look about them that spoke of business, not claim jumping. When they were twenty yards out, one of them hailed me.

"Halloo the camp!" he yelled. "May we ride in?"

"Come on in, gentlemen. What can we do for you?"

The two men dismounted. One was tall and slim and had the look of a banker. The other was shorter and stockier and wore a mustache. He could have been a cattleman. He was the one who did the talking. He offered his hand and I accepted it.

"My name is Wayne Jackson," he said. "My friend here is Frank Ganz." He looked around. "Nice setup you have here."

I shook hands with the second man, Ganz. Henry did likewise. As usual, Henry let me do the talking.

"Thanks. Charles E. Boles. Pleased, I'm sure. This gentleman here is Henry Roberts"

"Having any luck, Mr. Boles?" he asked.

I grunted. "If you count going backwards—but I guess bad luck is still luck."

Jackson ignored my humor and continued to look around. Then he looked at me directly.

"Well, perhaps you'll consider selling... Mr. Boles—Mr. Roberts, let me get right to the point. Mr. Ganz and I work for Wells, Fargo and company. We would like to buy your claim from you."

I thought for a moment, looking at Henry.

"We're not really in the market to sell, gentlemen, but thank you."

"Well, you haven't even heard our offer! How about $200.00?   That's a fair amount, especially if you're not having any luck…"

"No—thank you, really. We don't want to sell right now…"

The two of them looked at each other.

$250.00 then? You could live for a year on that."

I was starting to feel impatient.

"No thank you. Now, if you'll excuse us, we have to get back to work—"

Perturbed, the two men left.

Looking back, we probably should have taken their offer, *if* it was a real offer…

One of my favorite places to go, whenever I went into Silver Bow, was a restaurant that was operated by a Chinese man named Lee, his wife, and their two daughters. It served American food, unlike most places that were operated by Chinese. People from China kept mostly to themselves and had a tendency to be looked down upon, but Lee was different. He went out of his way to adopt American culture.

His daughters were named Mary and Frances. He was impeccably honest and his eyes were kind. His wife and daughters were both gracious and beautiful. I took an immediate liking to all of them and made a point to eat at their restaurant when I was in town.

I had been coming back to work every year now for more than six years. Danger was ever-present, but Henry and I had moved a couple of times, but we now had a claim that was continuing to pay us and we had made friends. My grief over losing my son the previous year was finally starting to subside, somewhat. Sometimes I could get through a whole day without feeling depressed. Some days were nearly happy again. Mary and I continued to write to each other and I still sent money to her and the girls, but our letters became less frequent and a little more formal.

Two weeks after my visit from Jackson and Ganz I awoke to a sobering surprise—there was no longer water flowing in our creek. Somehow, during the night or early that morning, something had happened that caused the creek to dry up. Henry and I looked about, puzzled and more than a little concerned. What could have caused this?

Without water, we couldn't work our claim. We would be finished here and would have to find another spot, in another place where water ran. There was still gold here, of that I was sure, but without water we couldn't extract it. How could this have happened?

From a deep puddle in the middle of the creek bed, I took enough water to make a pot of coffee and wash up. Then we had breakfast, although I had a knot in my stomach that made it hard to be hungry. Something was seriously wrong, here. I needed to find out what it was.

After breakfast, Henry and I picked up our rifles and began walking upstream. When we reached the Sweeney's camp, the two men were gone. Other men were there in their place. With a glance, I knew exactly what had happened.

They had diverted the creek. They had dammed it up and changed its direction. It now flowed to the north of where it had the day before, in a direction completely away from our claim.

One of the men working along the creek saw me and came walking over.

"Something I can do for you, gentlemen?" he asked.

"Where are the Sweeney brothers?" I demanded. "And why have you diverted the creek?"

"The Sweeneys are gone," he said. "They sold their claim to Wells Fargo. That's who I work for. I'm Hal Young. I'm the foreman here."

"Why did you change the direction of the creek?"

"Boss's orders. Wells and Fargo own that land over there. They want to see if there's any gold on it."

"You can't do that! We have a claim downstream and we need that water to work it! Without it, we're out of business!"

The foreman looked at the ground and made a face. Nodding, he looked back at me.

"Mister, let me ask you a question: Have a couple of men, named Jackson and Ganz, been by to see you in the last few weeks?"

"Yes—two weeks ago. Why?"

"Did they make you an offer?"

"Yes. We turned it down. Why are you asking me this?"

"It's how they work. When you turned the offer down, that told them you had something worth taking. All they had to do after that was go upstream, buy the land around you and—legally—divert the water onto their land and away from your claim. They've done it before and it always works. Others have tried to fight them on it and lost. I'm sorry."

I glared at him as the words sank in.

"And you…you work for these people?" I said derisively.

"Mister, it's a job and it pays. If I don't do it, somebody else will. I don't much like it sometimes, but I have a family and it pays the bills. My advice to you is to just pack up and find another creek to work in. What's done is done."

I continued to glare at him.

"And I suppose if we do find another good spot, they'll steal that too!"

"I am sorry, mister. Don't try to fight them. It'll just end up costing you. They have big city lawyers, and there's nothing in the law, says you can't divert a creek from one part of your property to another part of your property."

I glared at him for another thirty seconds.

"This isn't over," I told him. "Those sons of bitches don't know who they just messed with!"

Then I turned and walked back to what had only yesterday been a working, profitable gold claim. Our claim.

I spent about an hour walking in circles, wondering what to do. Realizing nothing *could* be done, I packed as much as I could carry and headed for town. Henry decided to stay at the claim for the time being. I never saw him again.

As I walked I felt rage and hatred and indignation grow inside me. I had done no wrong to any man. I had asked for nothing save the right to build and grow as others had. I had worked hard and kept to myself. I had served and fought to help make this country strong so that men like Wells and Fargo could prosper, had even been seriously wounded in the process. And what did I get for all my efforts, except to have what little I had stolen from me. How *dare* they?

Looking back, the rage I felt that day seems inordinate. It was like that old story about the man who piled too much straw on his camel's back. He piled on one straw too many one day and the camel's back broke. Somehow, all the pain and misery I had endured during the war, and the senseless, impotent grief I'd felt from losing my son, my crops—all of that seemed to get mixed into it.

I guess you might say something in me changed that day, something snapped. A sort of darkness that had been hiding inside me emerged and I could not send it back. Nor did I want to.

And long, long before I reached the town of Silver Bow, I swore to myself that somehow, *some way*, I would find a way to get even with Wells and Fargo, no matter how long it took. Not just for what they had done to me, but for what the world had done and had taken from me as well, and for what they had done to others like me.

The next day I wrote a letter to Mary and sent her half the money I had saved. I also told her of my intention to take revenge. "I will take steps," I wrote to her. "I will take steps…"

ELEVEN

I MADE UP my mind to tell no one else of my plans. In fact, at this point, I *had* no real plans, but I also had no doubt that, at some point, an opportunity would present itself to me. When it did I would be ready. I ate breakfast at Lee's restaurant one last time, said my goodbyes, then caught a stagecoach for Billings. For that entire trip, I was keenly aware of the strong box on top of the coach. That box contained gold that belonged to Wells and Fargo, gold they had stolen from me, and from others like me...

The railroad had gone through five years earlier, all the way to San Francisco. A trip from New York, which in the past had taken months, could now be done in four weeks. From Montana it took less than two. I got off the train at Illinoistown, which I had last seen twenty years earlier. When the railroad came through they had changed the name of the town, and it was now called "Colfax". The town was much changed, modernized, and no matter how hard I looked I could find no one who was around when I had lived there before.

I had no real plans at this point as to what I would do. The thought of prospecting irked me. Wells Fargo had people everywhere and did business from coast to coast, and the thought of letting them steal another claim from me was onerous. I caught the stage to Sacramento, again very much aware of the gold that was riding above me. When the train came through again, I caught it and went to San Francisco.

San Francisco—what a place! It had everything! Plays, restaurants, fashions…I saw wealth of a type I had never dreamed of before. I saw the best shows, dined in the finest restaurants, stayed in a grand hotel. It wasn't long before I was down to half of the money I had brought with me. It didn't matter. This was how I wanted to live. I would have to find a way to afford it, and I did.

Wells Fargo would provide it for me.

I took the train back to Colfax, then traveled thirteen miles north to the town of Grass Valley, then four more miles east to Nevada City, where I took a room at the National Hotel. While in San Francisco I had come up with a plan for what I was to do. Although Grass Valley and Nevada City were two of the richest gold towns in California, I would stay away from gold, gold mining and gold production of any kind. I wanted something that was simple and quiet, something that would meet my needs, arouse no suspicion and yet allow me to travel occasionally. I found it at the Reader Ranch, outside of Nevada City.

James Reader was a cattle rancher. He owned 900 acres of land, ten miles out of town. He also owned a sawmill and, word had it, might be in need of a mill operator. Working my way out of town, I walked up the road to his house and found him working in his barn, where I introduced myself as Charley Martin.

"Mr. Reader," I began. "My name is Charles E. Martin—Charley, to my friends. I heard in town that you might be looking for a mill operator. I'd like to apply for the position."

"Nice to meet you, Charley," he said. We shook hands and, as we did, he looked around. "Where is your horse?"

"I never much cottoned to horses, Mr. Reader, nor they to me."

"You walked all the way out here? From town?"

"Yes sir. I was part of the 116th Illinois Infantry Regiment, attached to General Sherman. Twenty miles a day was an easy stroll for us."

"Sherman—you must have seen some action…"

"My share and then some, sir. Got the scars to prove it."

He grunted. "What rank were you?"

"Joined as a private. Got promoted up to First Lieutenant. Got wounded at New Hope Church and they thought I would die, so they busted me back to First Sergeant so they wouldn't have to pay as much to my widow's pension. Mustered out in June of 1865, as First Sergeant."

Laughing, he said, "Sounds about right for the Army... Tell you what—it's lunchtime. Let's go on up to the house and have something to eat. You've got to be hungry, after that walk."

"I'd be much obliged, Mr. Reader," I told him.

"Call me Jim, Charley."

That was the first time I gave a false name to someone, but it would by far not be my last. I felt a little uncomfortable with it at first, but I soon got over it. Thereafter, I gave a different name at almost every town I entered. It later got to the point where each time I would re-enter a town I would have to ask myself, "Now, who am I to these people?"

Jim Reader was the kind of man that every man in his right mind aspires to be. He was strong, fair and honest. He had a motto:

"I do no man wrong, and no man does me wrong."

"I can respect that," I said. Over lunch he explained that, while he did need someone to work in the sawmill, it wasn't full time. Some days it would be, but most of the time it would only be a few hours a day. The job came with room and board and a small wage for the hours I did work. The work would pretty much end when winter came and then would start up again in the spring. If I wanted more work he could always use a little extra help with the cows.

"Well, like I said, I've never been much with horses or with cows, but I do know my way around a sawmill."

It was exactly what I was looking for. Even better, the "board" was not a bunkhouse, but a small cabin that sat about fifty yards from the sawmill. That meant I would have privacy.

During lunch we talked and he made the decision to hire me.

"Tell you what," he said. "Rather than head back to town now, why don't you get settled in over at the cabin and check out the mill. Tomorrow we can hitch up the buckboard and go into town and get your things—you can drive a buckboard, can't you?"

I assured him I could. After lunch he gave me blankets for the bed and a towel, took me up and showed me the cabin, then left me alone. I dusted the cabin and swept it out, then made up the bed. It was a simple, one room structure, and rustic, but I thought it was perfect and it had a great view. Later, I walked down to the sawmill and checked it out. It was simple enough, but it had everything I would need to mill whatever wood they required. Jim had also told me that he sometimes milled wood for others, so I might be kept busier than expected if there was much building going on. That was fine with me, too.

Late in the day, just as my stomach was starting to growl, I heard the dinner bell and walked up to the house.

Life at the Reader Ranch was, in many ways, idyllic. Some days I would work the whole day through, but most days I would work only a few hours, then spend the afternoon fishing in one of the creeks that ran through the property.

Then there were the days that I would get all my work done and disappear from the ranch for a few days to go exploring, or to take care of business. I made sure this was a pattern for me, so that no one found it odd when I would leave.

On July 26th, 1875 I was waiting at the top of Funk Hill, outside the town of Copperopolis, in Calaveras County. I wore a linen duster and had a flour sack over my head with holes cut out so that I could see. My twelve-gauge shotgun was loaded. Something about that didn't feel right. The driver and the passengers, whoever they were, had done me no wrong and my quarrel was not with them. I had seen enough carnage during the war and knew exactly what would happen if I unloaded the shotgun at anyone. The thought of that sickened me and the idea of harming someone who was innocent appalled me. I realized then that if that happened, I would end up turning myself in and would probably hang. War was something I'd had to do. This wasn't.

I unloaded the shotgun. Nor did I ever reload it again, when confronting a stagecoach. If I got injured or killed, then that was the price of my revenge. I would not bring harm to someone who had done me no wrong.

Strangely, unloading my shotgun gave me a sense of relief. I relaxed, and when the driver of the stagecoach came into view, I was ready for him.

TWELVE

I WAS STANDING in the center of the road, aiming my empty shotgun at the driver (a man named John Shine, who later became a U.S. Marshall and then a state Senator).

"Please throw down the box!" I requested. Over my shoulder I said, "If he shoots, give him a solid volley, boys!" I had placed sticks in the nearby trees, which at a glance looked like rifle barrels. I knew the shotgun would have his full attention. He quickly grabbed the box and threw it off the side of the coach. Then he threw down the mail sacks.

"Don't give them any trouble!" The driver told the people in the coach. One woman panicked and threw out her purse. Keeping the shotgun trained on the driver, I picked it up and gave it back to her.

"Madame, I do not wish your money," I told her. "In that respect I honor only the good offices of Wells Fargo!" Then, with a flourish, I waved them on. The driver drove off quickly.

Using a hatchet, I began opening the strongbox. Then I quickly stuffed the money and gold into one of the mail bags. While I was doing this a second coach suddenly appeared. Aiming the shotgun at the driver, I demanded that he, too, throw down the box.

"I don't have one," he told me. I waved him on. There was a strange, unwritten law back then, that if a driver told the robber he didn't have a box, the robber let him go. If the robber found out later that the driver had lied, the driver would be shot. I would never do that, but that was something he didn't know.

After the second coach was gone, I quickly began walking away, cross country and on foot. When I was safely away I counted the money—$348.00, with a little more hidden in the mail. Not a fortune, but enough for a man to live comfortably for a year.

Actually, the money was almost a secondary consideration. After all that had happened I had finally struck a blow against my enemies and I felt elated by it. I had taken back some of what they had stolen from me and had done it with an empty shotgun. What on earth could be better?

Later I would find that the two drivers, and men from the coaches, had doubled back to try to catch me. When they reached the point where the robbery had taken place they saw the rifles in the trees and froze. Then they realized that it was sticks that were pointed a them. I also later learned that one of the passengers, a miner, had pulled his pistol. Another passenger, who happened to be the owner of the coach, forced the pistol to the floor, telling the miner, "Do you want to get us all killed?"

The newspapers, after hearing that I had given the woman back her purse, called me the "Gentleman Bandit".

And far, far from feeling that I had done something wrong, I felt that I had done something very *right*.

The months after that first robbery were good ones. I stashed what I had taken under the floorboards of my cabin and left it there. I didn't need it. I had everything I wanted out on the ranch. I had work, food, shelter—and friends. The Reader family were good-natured, honest folk and they treated me well. I admired Jim Reader and he treated me, and all his crew, with respect. The Reader's had nine children, plus two that had died, making a total of eleven. Jim's son, Frank, was about the same age that my son, Arian would have been, had Arian lived. I formed an attachment for the boy. We often went fishing together in the afternoons when I wasn't working.

Suppertime at the ranch was always a social hour. Jim's cowboys had their own setup and their own cook, but I got to take my meals with the Readers. The food was always good, the conversations lively and fun. Afterward, I would sit on the porch of my cabin, have a smoke and read until the light was gone. I made sure to make regular trips away, both to establish a pattern and to gather information about gold shipments. I wanted the folks at the ranch to be used to my being away from time to time—and not just when robberies were committed.

In September I took $150.00 from my floorboard stash and went to San Francisco. I checked into the Palace Hotel under the name of Charles Bolton, and for that one week I literally lived like a king.

On December 28th, I held up the stage again, this time on the road from North San Juan to Smartsville, not many miles from the ranch. During the robbery I recognized one of the people on the coach and later realized it was only good fortune that he didn't recognize me as well. True, I wore my linen duster and flour sack disguise, but my eyes are blue and somewhat distinctive. I was lucky that the man on the stage never looked directly at me or I might have been caught. After that I traveled far and wide to perform my robberies, and only robbed the stage in Nevada County one other time.

I waited until the following June before hitting Wells Fargo a third time, this time in Siskiyou County, near the town of Cottonwood. This time I hit them at night. I wanted to do something different, so that Wells Fargo's Pinkerton detectives couldn't pin me to a particular pattern of attack. By this time I began to realize that I was actually having fun with this. I was getting even with the people that had stolen from me, true, but the pure excitement I felt each time I held up the stage was incredible. I was frightening people, I knew, but in that sense it was almost innocent fun. It was like jumping out of the dark and yelling "BOO!" at someone. Only I knew that my shotgun wasn't loaded and that I was actually harmless.

I began to look forward to each new robbery with great anticipation. The money was like a bonus.

The newspapers all posed the question of who I might be. I decided to give myself an identity...

On August 3rd, 1877 I held up the stage for the fourth time, this time in Sonoma County, near Fort Ross. I left behind a poem I had written:

"I'VE LABORED LONG AND HARD FOR
BREAD,
FOR HONOR AND FOR RICHES
BUT ON MY CORNS TOO LONG YOU'VE TREAD,
YOU FINE-HAIRED SONS-OF-BITCHES.
—BLACK BART, THE P O 8"

I took my time, crafting that poem. I knew that they had ways of identifying you by your handwriting, so I wrote each line in a different style and as unlike my own writing as I could make it. Years earlier I had read a story, *"The Case Of Summerfield"* in which the villain had an unruly black beard, dressed all in black and called himself Black Bart. When I was writing that poem the name of Black Bart jumped out at me, and I decided to use it. I found it ironic, since I never wore black and had light hair and eyes. If anything, I was the opposite of the Black Bart in the story. That suited me just fine.

At my fifth robbery I also left a poem. This took place in Butte County, near Berry Creek Sawmill:

"To wait the coming morrow,
Perhaps success, perhaps defeat
And everlasting sorrow.
Yet come what will, I'll try it once,
My conditions can't be worse,
But if there's money in that box,
It's munny in my purse.
—Black Bart, the P o 8"

This took place on July 25th, 1878, nearly a year after my fourth holdup. For awhile I wasn't sure if there would be a fifth robbery.

* The Case Of Summerfield by **William Henry Rhodes**

I had gotten lucky four times and had left them a clue, taunting them. Why push my luck? But after months of living the quiet life out at the ranch, I realized I could resist neither the excitement, nor the money. It's hard to say which of the two inspired me more.

That was the last time I would leave a poem, but it added to what was becoming my "legend". The newspapers loved it. They called me "The Plundering Poet".

I began to make small investments with the money I earned from my robberies, which brought me a residual income. Most of these would be confiscated later, but I made one investment—a big one—that they would never learn about.

Most of my days were spent out at the ranch, working in the sawmill, fishing or sitting on my porch, reading, enjoying my life there. The Readers became like a second family to me, one that I cherished.

Once or twice a year I would go to San Francisco, check into one of the finest hotels as "Charles Bolton", and live as well as a human being can. When people there became interested in where my money came from, I told them I was a mining engineer. A successful one.

In San Francisco, I generally stayed at the Palace Hotel, as it was one of the finest hotels around. On one of my visits there I met a man named Sam Brannan. Sam was an interesting man. Most people credited him with making San Francisco what it was, and was the town's first millionaire. He was Mormon, but he loved to drink and carouse. He had also created the resort town of Calistoga and had built a railroad just to take rich patrons there. I had supper with him one time. He pressed me to find out where exactly my mining interests were, so after that I avoided him. He also drank too much— something I could ill afford to do. Dropping my guard could easily lead to disaster for me. Letting slip the wrong word at the wrong time might well mean the end of Black Bart, and of Charles Bolton.

Two days after my fifth robbery I struck again, this time in Plumas County. I would hit Wells Fargo twice more that year, on October 2nd and 3rd and in Mendocino County. I had a project in mind at that time and I needed to raise money for it. I also wanted to spread myself around, leaving no particular pattern that the Pinkertons might learn to predict. It worked. They never knew when or where I might strike next.

One reason they never caught me was that they were always searching for someone on horseback. It never occurred to the authorities that a man might walk to and from a robbery. The infantry had taught me to "force march", and I put that practice into play each time I robbed a coach. I would walk 25 – 30 miles a day, both to and from the robberies. I would cover terrain that a horse would find difficult or downright impossible.

Shortly after my fourth robbery I made a pleasant discovery. I was walking on Commercial Street, in Nevada City, making my way through the Chinese quarter of the town. I happened to look through the window of a restaurant and saw Lee. I was genuinely happy to see him and he seemed just as happy to see me. By sheer coincidence he, along with his family, had moved to Nevada City and had opened a restaurant there.

Most whites had little to do with Chinese at that time. I had liked Lee and his wife from the moment I met them. Whenever I went into town after that day I would go by his restaurant and have a meal there, and we became great friends. That friendship would one day play an important role in my life, and one that no one else would ever learn of.

After my 7th and 8th robberies, which took place one day apart in Mendocino County, I took a break until the following June, when I once more held up the stage in Butte County, near Forbes Town. I would strike two more times that year, four times in 1880 and five times in 1881.

Eventually, I found my time away from the ranch to be such that, to avoid suspicion, I moved to San Francisco as a full-time resident. I took rooms at the Webb house, Number 37, on Second Street. My mining "cover" turned out to be perfect. As a mining engineer, Charles E. Bolton would spend much time traveling, and no one suspected a thing because of it.

I would occasionally go back to the ranch to visit, for they had become like family to me, and I would help with any milling that needed to be done. I came to look forward to those visits, especially to the time I knew would spend fishing with young Frank Reader.

THIRTEEN

ON JULY 13, 1882, I was waiting along the road near the town of LaPorte, in Plumas County. As the stagecoach approached I stepped into the middle of the road as always, and yelled, "Please throw down the box!" This time I got a surprise. The driver, a man named George Helms, had another man named George Hackett riding next to him. Reacting quickly, Hackett whipped his rifle up and shot me. The shot knocked my hat off and creased my skull, near the hairline and on the right side of my forehead. I ran into the woods and escaped, but I would forever have a scar from that encounter. I laid low for several days, nursing my wound out of sight from others. For a long time after that whenever I went out, I pulled my hat low on the right side of my head, to hide that scar. Later, if anyone asked, I told them I received it in the war between the states.

Other than that one incident, my robberies seemed to go off without a hitch. I waited for two months before striking again, this time in Shasta County, then again two months after that, near the town of Cloverdale, in

Sonoma County. Then I waited five months and hit that same spot again. After that I would have only one more successful holdup. Then my luck, as they say, ran out.

I had hit Wells Fargo twenty-seven times without giving them a clue as to who I really was. I suppose, looking back, that the law of averages was against me. Like a gambler that keeps gambling until he gives his winnings all back, I kept going. I had developed a style of life that suited me—I lived very well. My returns on my investments helped, but to keep living as I did required more. Robbing Wells Fargo covered that handsomely. In my heart, I knew my revenge on those people was complete, twice over, but I kept going. I kidded myself that I would quit after the number of holdups reached 30, or perhaps 50. Deep down I knew that, as long as I could walk and carry an empty shotgun, I would not stop.

November 3rd, 1883 was a pleasant day. The weather had just begun to turn cool, but that day was comfortable. I was at the top of Funk Hill, in Calaveras County. I had brought along some raisins and walnuts, and I nibbled on these while I waited for the stage to appear. At length I saw it appear far down the hill and was immediately concerned, for there was a young man sitting atop the stage, next to the driver. The last time there were two people up top it hadn't worked out well for me, and I still bore the scar from being shot at.

I debated on letting this one pass, then decided against it. The passenger sitting next to the driver had looked young. I would aim my shotgun at him and speak a little harsher than I normally would and hope to get my bluff in. I would also be ready to run if the kid didn't buy it. As an added precaution, I had taken the buckshot out of two shotgun shells and left it wrapped up in a handkerchief in my valise. If I had to fire back, the shotgun would at least make a loud "POP", even if nothing came out.

To my surprise (and no small alarm), when the stagecoach reached my spot, the driver was alone.

"Hold up!" I yelled to the driver, who immediately stopped the coach. "What happened to your passenger?"

"What passenger?" he asked.

"The man that was sitting next to you, ten minutes ago!"

"Jimmy Rolleri. He's out hunting. I dropped him off at the base of the hill. I'll pick him up on the other side."

I considered that for a moment. Then:

"Throw down the box!" I told him.

"Can't be done! Wells Fargo bolted it to the coach!"

This was getting to be aggravating.

"All right," I yelled. "Set your brake! Then climb down and disconnect your team. You won't be going anywhere until I have that box!"

He did as he was told. He then stood off to one side as I, using a wrench from the coach's toolbox, unbolted the strong box. This was taking much too long. I did not like it.

When I was done I threw the box to the ground, followed by the mailbag.

"All right!" I told the driver. "Hook your team back up and go!"

Minutes later, I watched the stagecoach disappear down the hill. I immediately began working to get the box open. Barely had I done so when something struck the strong box before me. A half-second later I heard the gunshot. I snapped up what was in the box and ran into the woods, getting away, but not before a bullet struck me in the hand.

I ran for about a quarter mile and then stopped. No one was following me and I needed to address my wounded hand, which was bleeding badly. Also, I felt strangely weak. Getting the strong box off the coach had been exhausting work. Maybe it was the blood I'd lost, but I suddenly felt like a child could take me down. I wrapped the wound as best I could in a handkerchief, and managed to get the bleeding stopped. I was painfully aware that, if they had wanted to follow me, I had left them an easy trail.

The bags from the strong box held nearly twenty pounds of gold amalgam and $500.00 in gold coins. I took the coins and stashed the bags with the amalgam under a rotted log. Then I put the shotgun into the hollow of a tree and moved on.

For the next couple of days I stayed in the woods and kept out of sight. At one point I found a hunter's cabin and staked it out. When I was sure no one was staying there I went in. During my escape I'd left a valise that held a number of personal items. I had also lost my hat. In the cabin I found a replacement hat, flour, salt and sugar—and coffee. Whoever lived in the cabin left behind no milk or eggs, but there was a nearby stream, so I had water. I built a fire in the stove, made coffee and poor-man's pancakes. After two days of running and being starved and cold, that cabin felt like the Palace Hotel.

The next morning I moved on, right after sunup. I headed west, knowing I would eventually find Sacramento. I happened across another cabin, but this one was occupied by an old miner who called himself "Old Martin". I asked him for directions to Coulterville, then moved off as if I was actually going there. After traveling south for a quarter mile, I turned west again and north, heading once more for Sacramento. I had taken a room there and had not checked out, thinking I would only be gone for one or two days. By now I was sure they would be wondering what had happened to me.

I walked into Sacramento five days after the robbery, going straight to a barber for a shave, a haircut and a bath. I also got fitted for a new suit. Then, after letting the hotel know I was still around, I caught the train to Reno. I stayed in Reno for a few days, then headed back to Sacramento, where I picked up my new suit and went on back to San Francisco. I didn't go directly to the Webb house, where my rooms were, but took a room for the night at a medium-priced hotel. Finally deciding there was nothing amiss, I returned to the Webb house and resumed my life as Charles Bolton.

Everything seemed fine at first and life went on as it had before. Then I stopped by my tobacconist, on Post Street, and there was a man waiting there who wanted to talk to me. Tom

Ware, the owner of the shop, introduced him as Hamilton.

"Are you Bolton, the mining man?" Hamilton asked me.

"Why yes, yes I am," I said. "What can I do for you?"

"I have heard of you. I have a mining matter of some importance that I was hoping to consult you on. If you could spare a few moments of your time I would be grateful to you—my office is but a short walk…"

"Of course," I told him. "Always happy to help out a fellow miner!"

As it turned out, Hamilton's office was about five blocks away, on Sansome Street. The sign above the door read "Wells Fargo". When we entered I immediately knew I was in trouble, but did my best not to show it. Hamilton showed me to a desk and asked me to sit down, then excused himself for a moment. I thought of leaving, then, but he came back quickly and he wasn't alone. I recognized the second man from pictures I had seen of him in the newspapers. James Hume was Pinkerton's lead detective. He was in charge of capturing Black Bart. In the past I had taunted him, telling the stagecoach drivers to "Give my regards to Mr. Hume" as I was holding them up.

My luck had finally run out.

Hume wasted no time.

"Mr. Bolton is it? I'm James Hume. I just have a few questions I wanted to ask you. Where, exactly, are your mines located? And what are the names of your mines?"

"Well," I began, "they're in the foothills, in a couple of different places."

"Yes, but, where exactly?"

"I'm not in the habit of giving out that information," I told him. "It's the kind of thing I like to keep private."

"I see." Then, pointing at my injured hand, he asked, "Would you mind telling me how you injured your hand?"

"A small accident while I was getting off the train, in Truckee, a few days ago. "

Hume nodded. Reaching into a desk drawer, he produced a handkerchief that looked like one of mine.

"Do you recognize this, Mr. Bolton?"

"It's a handkerchief... Just what is this about?"

"It's your handkerchief. It's got your laundry mark. It was found at the scene of a robbery that took place one week ago."

"This is preposterous!" I said with indignation." "I am not the only one whose things bear that mark. Others have their washing done at the same place. Somebody may have stolen the handkerchief from me, or I may have lost it and someone else found it. Do you take me for a stage robber? I never harmed anybody in all my life, and this is the first time that my character has ever been called into question."

"Yes, Mr. Bolton. That is exactly what I take you for. I take you to be Black Bart!"

They took me into custody and put me in a jail cell. Then they searched my rooms at the Webb House, where they found clothing that bore the same laundry mark as the handkerchief—F.X.O.7. They also found a bible Mary had given me as a present, which bore the inscription: "This precious Bible is presented to Charles E. Boles, First Sergeant Company B, 116th Illinois Volunteer Infantry, by his wife as a New Year's gift, God gives us hearts to which His—faith to believe. Decatur, Illinois, 1865."

The following morning, the man I had met as "Hamilton" and I headed for Stockton. His real name, I learned was Morse. Hume had hired him specifically to hunt me down.

Throughout it all I maintained that I was neither Black Bart, nor this Boles character. Later, it dawned on me that all my denials were doing me no good. At Stockton they managed to produce "Old Martin", who instantly identified me as the man who asked him for directions.

Things were looking bad for me and I knew it. Sensing that my resolve might be weakening, Morse threw out a carrot, of sorts.

"If a stage robber forced his accusers to take him to trial and he was found guilty of several robberies," he said, "a judge might well give him a maximum sentence. On the other hand, if a stage robber pleaded guilty to a single crime with which he was charged, then went on to make restitution, that probably would be taken into consideration by the judge."

"Suppose the man that did commit the robbery should do this," I asked. "Would it not be possible for him to get clear altogether?"

"No," Morse said. "The law does not look upon stage robbery lightly. A man who pleads guilty to robbery must expect a prison sentence. However, that would certainly be better than a trial and the possibility of spending the rest of his life behind bars."

I gave it some more thought. They had me on one robbery and one robbery alone, but if they were able to make a connection between that one and all the other robberies I had done, I might well die in prison. In the end, I decided to cooperate and hope for the court's mercy. I told them: "I want you to understand that I'm not going to San Quentin, I'll die first."

I took them to the spot on Funk Hill, where I had held the stage up, then to where I stashed the gold and the shotgun. I was held over at the nearby town of San Andreas. Because I confessed there was no need for a trial. Literally eighteen days after committing my last robbery, I began serving a six-year sentence at San Quentin prison—the exact place I'd said I wouldn't go.

I dreaded going into that place more than I dreaded going into battle during the war. I knew there would be trouble, and that I would be tested. I was fifty-five years old—far older that most of the inmates. They would think me easy prey. I would have to prove them wrong about that, otherwise my stay there would really be intolerable. I had been a wrestling champion in my youth, so I had some moves that would be unfamiliar to most of them, and the sooner I used them the easier my stay would be.

My second day in I got my opportunity. I was in the prison yard and keeping to myself. There was a group of men eyeing me harshly. One of them was a real bruiser—several inches taller than I, with heavy, rounded shoulders. I did my best to ignore him, but he wasn't having it. From the corner of my eye I watched him walk toward me. By the way he moved I could tell he intended violence.

I'm sure he expected me to cower and take a beating. If that happened I might be seriously hurt and I knew it. I waited until he was two steps away, then suddenly turned toward him, stepped in close and jabbed the fingers of my left hand into his eye sockets. He howled and turned away and I struck him as hard as I could on the back of the neck. A moment later he was face down in the dirt. My right forearm was on the back of his neck and I had his right arm bent behind him in a hammer lock. I could have broken his neck, but I broke his arm instead.

That got me one week in solitary confinement. When I got out of solitary, the others left me alone. I always expected the man whose arm I broke to try to get even with me, but instead we became friends.

Charles Dorsey was a cold-blooded murderer and robber. He was a lifer, meaning he had received a life sentence and would see no parole, ever. He said I'd gotten the jump on him—something no man had ever done before. He also said that if circumstances had been reversed he would have broken my neck. He seemed good-natured about it, but for a long time

I kept my guard up around him. To my surprise, his good will toward me was real.

Most of my days I worked as a clerk in the prison hospital. Looking back, I suppose it could have been worse than it was.

But prison is still prison.

FOURTEEN

I ENDED up serving four years and two months out of a six-year sentence. I walked out on January 21, 1888. The morning of my release the press was there. Don't ask me how they knew, but somehow they did. I had hoped they would have forgotten about me and let me just go my own way, but it simply wasn't meant to be.

The guards all wished me luck as I passed through the inner gates and made my way outside. The man on the outer gate was named Howard. He was in his early thirties, with a pretty young wife and two sons. Like most of the guards, he was tough and hardened to the ways of convicts. If you just did your time and didn't look for trouble, though, they would usually give a man a fair shake.

"You take care of yourself now, Charley," Howard said as he unlocked the gate for me. "And try to stay out of trouble."

"That I will do, Howard," I said to him, "and you take good care of that handsome young family of yours."

"I will. Good luck."

And with that, I walked out of San Quentin.

There were a half-dozen news reporters waiting to talk to me. As soon as I was through the gate they all rushed forward, all talking at once. I held up my hand to quiet them.

"How does it feel to be out of prison, Charley?" One of them asked.

"It feels damn good," I told the man.

"How's your health, Charley?" Another asked.

"My health is fine, sir," I said. "I have a slight cough, due to the dampness of this place, but other than that I am fit as could be."

"What are your plans now, Charley?"

"I intend to eat a big steak, drink some good whisky and smoke a cigar. After that I plan to find a nice front porch somewhere, where I can sit in a rocker and whittle."

"You're not going back to a life of crime?"

"No, I'm done with crime—I'm retired."

"Charley—would you give us a poem?"

I turned and stared sharply at the young reporter who had just spoken.

"Young man," I told him, "didn't you hear me just say that I was done with crime?"

The reporters all laughed.

"Good day, gentlemen," I said. Then I turned, walked off and left them there.

I was now fifty-nine years old. Nearly everything I owned was in the valise I carried. As I walked, a couple of the reporters offered me rides. I thanked them politely, but declined. I had no desire for any kind of one-on-one interview with anyone from a newspaper. I wanted them to forget about me, and to be able to get on with my life.

Besides, that, I needed to walk. Life within the confines of San Quentin had left me on the soft side. There was no time like the present for me to begin getting my stride back. I walked the nine miles to Sausalito and caught the ferry to San Francisco, very much aware of the two Pinkerton men who were following me.

In San Francisco I meandered for a bit, enjoying the sights and sounds, and the smell of the bay. Then I made my way to The Nevada House, at 132 Sixth Street. The Nevada House was a four-story building, with 38 rooms and a restaurant on the bottom floor. There is also a lobby where guests can sit and relax.

You know, the Chinese have been much maligned in this culture, and treated poorly. I have found that, if you treat them fairly, you can have a friend for life. Take Lee, for instance. In 1880, I bought The Nevada House under the name of Samuel Hancock. I gave it its name, then gave half of it to Lee and his family to run as their own. My real name is on no paperwork, so there was never anything for Wells Fargo to confiscate. I always knew Lee would give me my half of whatever profits there might be, and Lee always came through.

In 1885, while still in prison and fearing that the authorities might somehow divine who Sam Hancock really was, I sold my "half" of the hotel. I did this through a third party and to an old friend, Eleonor Burling, with the provision that Lee be allowed to continue running the establishment and that he would get first refusal if she ever decided to sell. I would have sold it to Lee straight out, but hotels with European named owners did far better than those who were non-European, especially in that part of the city.

We conducted the deal completely under the noses of the prison guards, who had no clue about the transaction.

Mrs. Lee was the first to see me when I entered the restaurant. Her eyes grew wide and she literally ran to me, stopping just short of actually touching me, so as not to be impolite. Then Lee came to see what the commotion was. He rushed forward and we shook hands, like the timeless friends that we were.

"Do you happen to have a room available for an old man?" I asked him.

"For you, the BEST room!" he told me. Then he led the way, while I followed.

After spending the last four years in a four-by-eight cell, the room Lee gave me seemed palatial. It was large and well-appointed, with a large window that looked down on the street from the second floor. Lee got me settled in, then left. A few minutes later he knocked on the door and I let him in. He was carrying a valise. With both hands, he held it out to me, and I accepted it.

The valise was stuffed with hundred dollar bills and gold coins.

"It appears that business has been good for the past four years," I said.

"Yes! Very good!" he said, smiling.

Withdrawing $100.00 from the valise, I said, "Lee, I was wondering if I could ask you one more favor? Keep holding this for me while I'm here. There are people out there—if they thought I had this, they would break in and steal it."

Lee accepted the valise, bowed and left.

The Pinkertons believe I have only the small stipend that was given to me when I left the prison. They are also sure I have something stashed somewhere and will do their best to be there when I go for it.

Before I was caught I avoided The Nevada House. Lee and I would arrange a meeting once a month and he would pass me whatever I had coming. I never questioned what Lee gave me or asked for any kind of accounting. This place was his, fair and square. I wanted it in place only in case of an emergency.

Like this one.

Once more I settled into the life of a gentleman of leisure, albeit quietly. I took most of my meals at the Nevada House. After breakfast I would usually go out for the day and come back in the afternoon. The Pinkertons were always there, shadowing me. I intentionally pretended not to see them, but it pretty obvious for anyone with eyes. I kept my spending to a minimum, not wanting them to think I had anything but the small amount of money given to me when I left San Quentin. They were sure I had money stashed somewhere and planned on being there when I went for it. I was sure that they were not above breaking into my room, if they thought I had money stashed there.

It was not only the Pinkertons I had to be wary of. Others there were, who would stop at nothing if it might mean getting their hands on "Black Bart's Treasure". One afternoon while I was sitting and reading the newspaper, I ran across an ad:

Black Bart will hear something to his advantage by sending his address to M.R. Box 29, this office

This was an obvious ruse by someone to gain my whereabouts, one I had no intention of answering.

Usually I let the Pinkertons follow me and pretended not to see them, but a few days after my release I eluded them. Once I was certain that they were no longer behind me I went straight to a store and bought a new .41 Colt Thunder, a dual-action pistol that you didn't have to cock, just pull the trigger. I kept this with me at all times and, unlike my shotgun, I kept it loaded.

For more than a month I followed pretty much the same routine, letting the detectives waste their time watching me. The Pinkertons bill themselves as the greatest detectives in the world, but I was not greatly impressed by them. I robbed Wells Fargo twenty-seven times and they had not a clue as to my identity. It was only bad luck on my part (or the law of averages), that they caught me when they did.

I did write to Mary several times. In one of the letters I complained that the Pinkertons were everywhere and that I was demoralized by their constant attentions. I was fairly certain that letter would be intercepted and read before it reached her. It was a legitimate complaint, but I also wanted to give the detectives a false sense of confidence. That was the last time I would ever write to her directly. From then on I would send her letters and money through her cousin, Walter.

I was certain the Pinkerton detectives would not be canvassing his mail.

Late in February I finally made my move. By now the Pinkertons had to be wondering how I was getting by, since I had not worked since leaving prison, several weeks earlier. That morning I rose and ate breakfast, then said my goodbyes to Lee and his wife. I left the Nevada House as I had on other days, followed as always by the Pinkerton detectives. Since I almost never tried to elude the detectives, they weren't expecting it when I did.

Once I was certain they were no longer behind me, I headed for the train station and caught the train to Sacramento. From there I headed south. On February 27th, I checked into the Visalia House Hotel as Charles Bolton and paid for three nights. The next morning I ate breakfast. Then I left the hotel and did not return. I intentionally left a valise in my room which contained, among other things, cuffs that had my laundry mark on them—F.X.O.7—the same laundry mark that had tied me to the robbery at Copperopolis. I had left a trail that even the Pinkertons could follow, certain it would eventually lead them to the hotel in Visalia.

Then I started walking north.

I had taken my time getting to Visalia. I had bought supplies along the way—a bedroll, a coffee pot, a fry pan and a small cooking pot, and some canned goods. These I had stashed under some bushes in a dry creek bed, ten miles north of that town. When I checked in at the Visalia House I wanted nothing with me that might give my plans away.

My supplies were right where I'd left them. I collected them and then again headed north and slightly east, walking cross-country. I took great pains, especially on that first day, to make sure that I wasn't followed. The Pinkertons would follow the trail I had left heading south, and that's where I wanted them to keep looking for me.

That night I made my camp in a wooded area, next to a small creek and under the stars. I was miles from civilization. I had a small fire, coffee, and a supper of corned beef and crackers. I loved being out in the open air, and the smell of wood smoke. During my time in prison, this was something I had greatly missed. Being the first part of March, it was chilly out, but I was ready for that. Aside from being a little stiff with age, I had a comfortable night.

I figured it would take me roughly two weeks to get where I was heading. I would avoid people whenever I could. I have been told that I have distinctive blue eyes and a deep, clear voice. These can be a handicap when you want to travel unnoticed. Reason McConnell, the stage driver I had robbed at Copperopolis, identified me by my speech. It would do me well to remain unseen and to speak to no one until I got to my destination.

There was also another reason for avoiding people—I had thousands of dollars sewed into the lining of my coat and three-hundred dollars in gold in my pockets. Many men have been killed for far less.

FIFTEEN

I HAD just finished brewing my morning coffee, when instinct warned me to get out of sight. I ducked into some nearby bushes, pulled my Colt and waited. Moments later an old prospector leading a mule came into view. He stopped just outside the camp and waited.

"Halloo the camp!" he hollered.

I waited and said nothing.

"Halloo the camp!" he repeated. " Name's Vern Fallan! I'm alone, it's just me an' my mule. We're alone and friendly, but I sure could use a cup of that coffee. Smells darn good!"

Without leaving my cover, I told him, "Go ahead, help yourself!"

I watched him retrieve a cup from one of his saddlebags. Then he walked to the fire and filled the cup from my coffee pot.

"I can't speak for my mule," he said looking toward the woods where I hid, " but I'm fairly harmless. Haven't had a body to talk to for a few days now…"

I walked out of the woods, still holding my pistol.

"Can't be too careful, these days," I told him. "My name's Charley."

"I know what you mean. My name is Vern Fallan. My mule's name is Apple."

"Apple?"

"Yes. She was born in an apple orchard—and she does like apples..."

"Well, nice to meet you, Vern, Apple."

"I haven't had a cup of coffee in three days. Hits the spot."

"Where you headed?"

"Figured I'd do some prospecting a little south of here. Apple here tells me I might get lucky if I travel down to the southwest corner of Mariposa County. Apple knows how to find gold. Apple knows lots of things, but she only tells me."

I couldn't help but smile a bit.

"Well, she's quite a mule," I told him.

"Yes. Yes she is. She knows lots of things. She told me some things about you, when we was approachin' your camp."

I looked at Apple. She looked like an ordinary mule, if you believe mules can be ordinary.

"What did she tell you about me?" I asked him.

"She told me you were on the run—but, you haven't really done anything wrong. She said you're trying to get home, or at least the place you feel is home, only you're not sure the people there will accept you back when you get there. She said to tell you to relax. You'll be fine. Those are your people."

"She told you all that…"

"Yup! Well, I gotta be headin' on. Thanks for the coffee, Mr. Bart."

"It's Charley…" I said warily.

"Yes, but you're also Black Bart. Apple told me. She said not to worry. Everything will work out just fine. You'll see. Those are your people."

I had my hand on my pistol as I watched him leave. My eyes were on him and on everything else around me at the same time.

"I wish I could be sure of that…" I said quietly.

From the cover of the trees I watched him disappear out of sight. Every nerve in my body seemed to be tingling and I was on high alert. For days now I had kept away from people, moving through the countryside and avoiding folks whenever I could. Twice I had gone into mining camps and bought food. When I'd done that I'd spoken little and avoided eye contact. I was sure I hadn't seen Vern or Apple in either of those camps, but I suppose it was possible that he had seen me. Some newspapers had printed pictures of me, both upon my arrest and at my release. It was possible Vern had seen those pictures and recognized me, but how could he possibly know of my concerns?

I immediately broke camp and moved out, spooked by what had happened. I moved quickly for the next few hours, but lost time backtracking to make sure no one was behind me.

I made camp early that afternoon. The sky had begun to get darker and darker as I walked and I was sure a storm was brewing. One thing I carried with me was a large piece of canvas which, up until now, I had laid my bedroll on for insulation and to keep it dry. Now I stretched it out and hung it between two trees, so that it would be both over and under me, and hoped it would keep me dry. During the war I had spent many days when I was both cold and wet. I had no desire to repeat that experience now.

When my shelter was complete I made a fire, made coffee and sat on a nearby boulder, and waited for the coming storm. I was in good health, but I was also aware that I was no longer young. To be cold and wet at this age could be a dangerous thing, even deadly.

Then I had a comical thought. It would be a godlike irony if I were to get sick and die out here, alone, with over four thousand dollars stitched into my coat and hundreds of dollars in my pockets. Hopefully, that wouldn't happen.

I was still a little spooked by my encounter with Vern and Apple, but I was certain no one had followed me. I was also fascinated by the things he had told me, and I hoped he was right. The people I was going to see were good, honest folk. They had accepted me and trusted me as one of their own, and I had deceived them. That was the simple truth of it. I deceived them. There was no way in heaven for me to know how they would react when they saw me again, but I had to find out.

I awoke in utter silence. It was not yet sunup and the stars were brilliantly out. The reflection of them on four inches of fresh snow created a beautiful, blue-white landscape around me. I pulled my bedroll tighter about me and went back to sleep, happy to be warm, safe and dry.

SIXTEEN

NEVADA CITY was exactly as I remembered it. I walked into town in mid-afternoon in the middle of March, filled with both nostalgia and trepidation. Everything I had done up until now could easily be undone if word got back to the Pinkertons of my whereabouts. People here knew me and by now, would know of my other life. All it would take was one person to talk to a newspaper reporter and everything I had planned would be lost. Yet, this was something I had to do.

When the Pinkertons arrested me I was living in San Francisco. If they had dug deeper into my life they might easily have found out about Nevada City. Having captured me and obtained a confession from me, they didn't bother. If they had, then all of my efforts of the last couple of weeks may have been for naught. They would only have had to send one of their agents here to wait for me to show up and they would have me again. I'm taking a chance that *that* hasn't happened.

Nervous? Hell, yes. I was nervous as a cat!

For years I lived and worked with these people. When I wasn't living high in San Francisco as Charles Bolton I was here, working in the sawmill out at Jim Reader's Ranch. The people here are good, honest folk. In a way, I lied to them. They thought I was just plain, simple Charley—a guy who worked in a sawmill, but that whole time I was also holding up the Wells Fargo stage and living another life. True, I never took from the passengers. I always made it clear that my business was with Well Fargo. Also true, in twenty-eight holdups, I never once loaded my shotgun. The newspapers made much of those facts and referred to me as "The Gentleman Bandit", so if they know anything about me being Black Bart, they should know that.

But that doesn't mean those folks would take me back in. All I could hope for was that Vern's mule Apple was right.

It was a Saturday. I had planned to come into town that day and I also planned the time of day that I would arrive. I knew Jim Reader's habits and knew that, on most Saturdays, he would come into town, pick up whatever supplies he needed, then go to the

National Hotel Saloon for some socializing.

I had considered going around Nevada City altogether and just going on out to the Reader ranch. That would minimize my exposure, true enough, but it would also mean walking an extra twelve miles to get the answer I needed, and I was tired. I was tired of walking, I was tired of being alone, and I was tired of being on the run when I had already paid my debt to society. I also wanted a good cigar and a glass of whiskey. Either what Vern told me was right and they would accept me, or they would not. In either event, I would not be here long. I would make my peace today or not, then be on my way.

Still, a lot depended on just how this went.

I walked along Little Deer Creek until I came to Broad Street, crossed the bridge and walked up the short hill to the National Hotel. At the saloon door I stood, just breathing. I suddenly realized that, of all the things I've done and had to do in my life, this was going to be one of the hardest. There were people in the saloon, I was sure, that I had once considered good friends, and I had no way of knowing if they would accept me back or tar and feather me. Part of me wanted to just turn around and walk away, but I couldn't. This was something I needed to do. I took a deep breath, let it out and went in.

At first no one recognized me. I walked up to the bar. The bartender was a tall, sandy-haired man named Stuckey. When he saw me his eyes grew wide. Then he smiled.

"Whisky?" I asked him. He poured a double shot into a glass and pushed it across the bar to me.

"On the house, Charley," he told me.

"Thanks, Stuckey," I said. I drank half of it down, enjoying both the flavor and the burn.

Slowly, the conversation in the room began to die, until the room was completely quiet. Then someone began to clap. A moment later the entire room erupted in applause. I felt my face flush hot and felt strangely emotional. Slowly, I managed to look around the room and nodded to all the familiar faces.

Jim Reader was there, smiling and also applauding me. I walked over to him.

"Welcome home, Charley," he said.

I thanked him.

"Mr. Reader—" I began.

"It's Jim, Charley. It's always been Jim."

"Jim...the last time I visited the ranch, I left a few things. I was wondering if I might stop by and collect them?"

Jim Reader smiled a big, knowing smile.

"Of course, Charley. Whatever you left at the ranch is still there, waiting for you. In fact, I'll be heading out, shortly. You can ride back with me, have supper and spend the night. The missus and the kids will be glad to see you, especially Frank."

"That...would be wonderful," I told him.

And with that, we shook hands.

I would spend one more joyously happy night, celebrating with people who were like family to me. Then, tomorrow, Black Bart would disappear forever.

You know, life is funny

In almost every situation, there are two roads. One road will lead to power, the other away.

Always choose power...

"I've labored long and hard for bread,
For honor and for riches
But on my corns too long you've tread,
You fine-haired sons-of-bitches.

—Black Bart, the P o 8"

THE END

*AFTER LEAVING THE READER RANCH, Charley was never heard from in California again and the Pinkertons eventually gave up looking for him. In 1892 Mary listed herself as the widow of Charles E. Boles. She passed away in Hannibal, Missouri in 1896.

In 1917, a New York newspaper allegedly published an obituary for a "Charles E. Boles, Civil War veteran". Charley would have been 88 years old.

THE NEVADA HOUSE, at 132 Sixth Street in San Francisco, collapsed in the 1906 San Francisco earthquake, killing over 40 people, including most of the Lee family. Only Lee's son, Frank Lee, and six others survived. In the article *"I Was Buried In Complete Darkness"* fellow survivor William Stehr describes crawling out of that wreckage. The Nevada House was never rebuilt.

THE 900-ACRE READER RANCH, established in 1854, is still in operation today and is run by James Reader's descendants. The sawmill and Charley's cabin are both gone, but herding cattle is still the main occupation on the ranch.

Beginning on August 31, 1977 the Nevada County Independent Newspaper ran a three-part feature story written by the late Bob Paine, which told of the connection between James Reader and Black Bart, whom they knew as Charley Martin. It was from that story and from the recollections of Reader's great-grandson, Fred Langdon, that I based the ending of this book.

*Charles E. Boles AKA Black Bart

ROBBERIES:

1. **July 26, 1875**. Calaveras County at Funk Hill; Wells Fargo box and mail. Driver: John Shine.

2. **December 28, 1875**. Yuba County, four miles from Smartville. Wells Fargo box and mail. Driver: Mike Hogan.

3. **June 2, 1876**. Siskiou County, five miles north of Cottonwood; Wells Fargo Box and mail; a nighttime robbery. Driver: A.C. Adams.

4. **August 3, 1877**. Sonoma County, four miles from Fort Ross; Wells Fargo box and mail; first poem left here. Driver: Milt Watson or George Brereton.

5. **July 25, 1878**. Butte County, one mile from Berry Creek Sawmill; Wells Fargo box and mail; second poem left here. Driver: Ash Williamson or Jack Morrison.

6. **July 30, 1878**. Plumas County, five miles from LaPorte; Wells Fargo box and mail. Driver: D.E. Barry.

7. **October 2, 1878**. Mendocino County, twelve miles from Ukiah;

Wells Fargo box and mail. Driver: Alec Fowler.

8. **October 3, 1878**. Mendocino County, ten miles from Potter Valley; Wells Fargo box and mail. Driver: Nate Waltrip.

9. **June 21, 1879**. Butte County, three miles from Forbes Town; Wells Fargo box and mail. Driver: Dave Quadlin

10. **October 25, 1879**. Shasta County, enroute to Buckeye; Wells Fargo box and mail; nighttime robbery. Driver: Jim Smithson.

11. **October 27, 1879**. Shasta County, twelve miles from Millville; Wells Fargo Box and mail. Driver: Ed Payne.

12. **September 1, 1880**. Shasta County, near Last Chance Station; Wells Fargo Box and mail. Driver: Charles Cramer.

13. **September 16, 1880**. Jackson County, Oregon one mile from California line; Wells Fargo box and mail; nighttime robbery. Driver: Nort Eddings.

14. **September 23, 1880**. Jackson County, Oregon three mile from California state line; Wells Fargo box and mail. Driver: George Chase.

15. **November 20, 1880**. Siskiyou County, one mile from Oregon border; Wells Fargo box and mail. Driver: Joe Mason.

16. **August 31, 1881**. Siskiyou County, ten miles from Yreka; Wells Fargo box and mail. Driver: John Sullaway.

17. **October 8, 1881**. Shasta County, fourteen miles from Redding; Wells Fargo box; nighttime robbery. Driver: Horace Williams.

18. **October 11, 1881**. Shasta County, at Montgomery Creek; Wells Fargo box. Driver: Lewis Brewster.

19. **December 15, 1881**. Yuba County, four miles east of Dobbins; Wells Fargo box and mail. Driver: George Sharpe.

20. **December 27,1881**. Nevada County, at Bridgeport; Wells Fargo box and mail. Driver: Luther Sherman.

21. **21 January 26, 1882** Mendocino County, six miles from Cloverdale; Wells Fargo box and mail. Driver: Harry Forse.

22. **June 14, 1882**. Mendocino County, two miles from Little Lake; Wells Fargo box and mail. Driver: Thomas B. Forse.

23. **July 13, 1882** [1]. Plumas County, five miles from LaPorte; Bart shot; nothing taken. Driver: George Helms, Messenger: George W. Hackett.

24. **September 17, 1882**. Shasta County, at Bass Hill; Wells Fargo box and mail. Driver: Horace Willims.

25. **November 23, 1882**. Sonoma County, five miles from Cloverdale; Wells Fargo box and mail. Driver: Dick Crawford.

26. **April 12, 1883**. Sonoma County, five miles from Cloverdale; Wells Fargo box and mail. Driver: Bill Connibeck.

27. **June 23, 1883**. Amador County, four miles from Jackson; Wells Fargo Box and mail. Driver: Clint Radcliffe.

28. **November 3, 1883**. Calaveras County, at Funk Hill; Wells Fargo box and mail; Bart shot. Driver: Reason E. McConnell.

*List of robberies provided by Lynn Woodward at blackbart.com

Taken From: *Three Fearful Days: San Francisco Memoirs of the 1906 earthquake & fire—by Malcolm E. Barker*

"I Was Buried and in Complete Darkness"

By William Stehr

The area most devastated during the initial earthquake was a cluster of inexpensive hotels and rooming houses in the South of Market

**Street area. William Stehr lived on the top
floor of the Nevada House at 132 Sixth Street.**

I jumped out of my bed and ran to the window
and opened it. My room was on the top floor and
the window faced south, overlooking the roof of
the Ohio House and the Brunswick Hotel beyond
it on Sixth Street. By the time I got the window
opened, the shaking had grown worse. I was not
yet thoroughly awake but I was considerably
alarmed, and my first thought was, "My! But this
is a heavy quake!"

It came into my head to jump out of the window
on to the roof below; but while I was waiting to
make up my mind the house I was looking at
collapsed with a deafening roar and spilled down
in a cloud of dust from which I could plainly hear
the agonizing screams of the [tenants]. The dust
then came spurting up in so thick a cloud that I
could neither see nor breathe. It choked me. So I
hurried back from the window to the other end of
the room and began to dress myself.

I had just got on my trousers and shoes when I
heard another crash. Looking out again through
the window I saw that the Brunswick House, the
second building south of us, on the corner of
Sixth and Howard streets, had also collapsed, and
was tumbling into a heap of ruins in a smother of
dust. This building was said to have been
occupied by 150 people, of whom only fifty
escaped with their lives.

I did not put on any more clothes, but jumped up and tried to open the door of my room and get out. But I found that I could not open it. The earthquake had jammed the door, and every jerk of the quake made it faster and tighter. As I was tugging at it I felt the floor tilting and sinking under me, and I knew that the house was going down like the others. So I hung on instinctively to the door handle while the whole floor dropped. As it sank I felt three distinct bumps as the lower floors collapsed in turn under the weight of the roof and the top story. With each bump came a frightful crash and cracking of timbers and glass and the cries of other people in the house who were being destroyed.

There were about fifty people in the Nevada at that moment, and of these only seven escaped, including myself. The landlord, Mr. Lee, his wife and daughter were among those that perished, but his young son Frank was among those saved.

The cries of these people who were being killed, especially the women, were dreadful to hear; even to me, in my own peril, thinking every instant that I would be crushed, they were the most dreadful part of the experience.

Then came another bump, very sudden and very severe. The place fell in on top of me, the breath seemed to be knocked out of my body and I went unconscious. When my senses came back I was buried and in complete darkness. I tried to feel myself all over, working my limbs as best I could, to find out if any bones were broken. But though I could feel that I was painfully bruised all over, I guessed that all my bones were intact.

Then I tried to raise myself, because when I came to I was lying flat; but the weight of the debris that covered my body was more than I could lift. My feet were pinned fast, so I ceased struggling and rested for a minute or so. While I was gasping for more breath for a second struggle I heard somebody running over the debris above me, so I shouted for help as loudly as I could. No attention was paid to my calls; so I began to struggle again, and presently managed to release my feet. But I lost my left shoe. It was wedged in too tight, and it was by pulling my foot out of it that I escaped.

After that I began to grope and feel about me to find some way of escape. Then I began to hear other agonizing screams for help, and screams of "Fire!" And soon after I began to smell smoke, and I fancied I could hear flames crackling sharply. This made me struggle desperately, and soon I got my arms out over my head, and could feel an opening that led upwards on a slope. I worked my way along till I could see a little glimmer of light. I got to the crack in the debris and could see out; but I was in a very tight place and was very tired from the exertion, so I had to stop for a while. But I got a breath of fresh air which revived me, and I began to cough violently and spit out the dust and plaster with which my mouth and lungs seemed to be filled.

After resting for a minute or so, as well as I could judge, I began to pull away the laths and plaster that blocked the passage. It was hard work doing it in such a tight and narrow passage. But after a while I made a hole large enough to crawl through, and then I found that I was not at the end of my trouble. I had to turn on my back and crawl upward through a sort of chimney that was bristling with nails and splinters of laths and plaster that tore my sides and my clothes. But eventually I squeezed through and found myself sitting amid the ruins nearly on a level with the street, and all around me was ruin and debris.

I was too exhausted to mind much, and I was bleeding badly from a cut over the scalp. As the blood was running into my eyes, the first thing I did was to sit on the debris and tie my handkerchief around the cut on my head to staunch it. Then I looked at my watch, which was still going. It was 5:45 o'clock. As I was sitting there, trembling and trying to collect my scattered senses, a man that I don't think I ever saw before or since climbed up beside me with a bottle of whisky and told me to take a drink. I took it and thanked him. It made me feel much better. Then he went off with the bottle to give a drink to somebody else.

Soon I began to take enough interest in things to look about me. On all sides, where the Nevada, the Ohio, the Brunswick and other lodging houses had been, there was nothing but a big pile of debris. On this pile a number of men were working desperately trying to rescue people that were buried. Some of these men were armed with axes and hatchets, but the majority had nothing but their bare hands to work with.

For some time I was too exhausted to stand up, much less try to help them. I just watched while they dragged at the broken timbers and things, while smoke kept puffing up among them from the fires that had started underneath. Then I began to hear again the cries and shrieks that I had for a time ceased for a time to notice. It was very dreadful when someone gave a long agonizing scream when the fire caught him, and then ceased.

But the rescuers kept on working in each spot until the fire drove them back. Wherever they heard a voice or a cry they started to dig down to it; but in most cases the victims were too deeply buried, and the flames drove away the rescuers while the victim perished.

The above is an extract of an account taken from Malcolm E. Barker's book, *Three Fearful Days: San Francisco Memoirs of the 1906 earthquake & fire* (Londonborn

Publications, San Francisco, 1998), and was originally published in 1926 by *The Argonaut*.

Used by permission.

SOURCES:

Susan Goldstein and Sylvia Rowan—San Francisco History Center

Lynn Woodward—blackbart.com

Fred Langdon—James Reader's great grandson

Wickipedia.org

Buried In Darkness by William Stehr

Mycivilwar.com

Civilwar.org

Sources: Civil War Album, Steele's Bayou Expedition,

Sonofthesouth.net, http//civilwar.illinois.org

Crossing The Plains In '49 by G.W. Thissell

Aaron Seltzer
Archives Specialist
National Archives At San Francisco

The Nevada County Independent

The Doris Foley Historical Research Library in Nevada City, CA

PRAISE FOR "HUGH GLASS"
by Bruce Bradley—

Editorial Review— "...a great read and should be added to the library of those who have interest in American History." —On The Trail Magazine

Editorial Review— "...The kind of book you hate to put down!" —Fraser Whitbread, Muzzle Blasts Magazine

175 REVIEWS—*AVERAGE REVIEW 4.5 STARS*

Four Stars—

"…It's a very readable telling of an amazing story. "—Bob Griffith, Amazon.com Reviews

Four Stars—

"Enjoyable read. I have heard so much about Hugh Glass and knew of his name and some of his history, but not the full account. The man was a true man, with all of the colorful past that most Mountain Men had." —John Oliver, Amazon.com Reviews

Five Stars—

"Hard to put down!"   —G. Sporer, Amazon.com Reviews

Five Stars—

"Really enjoyed it!" —Raymond Glass, Amazon.com Reviews

Five Stars—

"You can tell that Bradley spent a lot of time researching this book between the details he uses, sailing, and Indian customs among other things. He definitely is a storyteller and a wonderful writer as well. Great book for any Hugh Glass fans or those wanting to learn more!"—Courtney, Amazon.com Reviews

Four Stars—

"I would highly recommend this book!" —Joanie B., Amazon.com Reviews

THIS IS THE TRUE STORY THAT INSPIRED THE MOVIE *"THE REVENANT"!*

BOOK EXCERPT—

HUGH GLASS

By Bruce Bradley

On the third morning after the attack by the Mandans, Hugh woke up feeling uncomfortable and out of sorts. He had slept wrong, and he'd had some unsettling dreams about Little Feather. He couldn't remember the dreams, only that she had been in them. It left him in a somber mood.

He reached the camp in time for coffee and a biscuit. While he was eating, young Jim Bridger approached him. Hugh liked Bridger. The young man talked very little, but he handled himself better than most men who were ten years older. What Hugh really wanted right now, though, was to be left alone.

"Mr. Glass...?" Bridger said tentatively.

"Mornin' Jim," Hugh said. "What can I do for you?"

Bridger looked around awkwardly. He wanted something from Hugh, but he hated to ask.

"Mr. Glass, is it true you know how to read sign, the way the Indians do?"

"Yes," Hugh told him. "I can read sign."

"Well...I was wonderin'.... Could you, maybe, teach me? I-I can pay. I'll pay you. I don't expect nothin' for free."

Hugh immediately thought of Big Axe. His mood softened somewhat. He smiled.

"You don't have to pay me," he said. "I'll be happy to teach you, as soon as we get to Fort

Henry."

"Is there some...some secret to it? I mean, I can tell what tracks *are*, when I can see 'em. Trouble is, they always disappear."

Hugh scratched the back of his neck. Looking up at Bridger, he said, "Yeah, there is a secret. You have to learn to soften your eyes."

Bridger looked puzzled. It made him look even younger than he was. It made Hugh think of his own sons, whom he had not seen in more than six years and who, he knew, he would almost certainly never see again.

Hugh threw the dregs of his coffee into the fire.

"Come on," he told the younger man. "We have a few minutes. I can show you enough to get you started."

He led Bridger over to a spot just past the edge of the camp, to a stand of cottonwoods. Casting about for only a moment, Hugh pointed at a pile of leaves.

"What do you see there?" he asked Jim.

"Leaves," Jim said. "Just leaves."

Getting down on one knee, Hugh looked at the pile.

"I see three different sets of tracks," he told Jim. "Over here—" He pointed to a spot just to his left. "—you can see where a fox followed a rabbit, probably yesterday. He wasn't chasing the rabbit yet, just following. Then, over here on the right, you can see where a prairie chicken walked through, scratching around, lookin' for *his* dinner."

"But how...?"

"You have to teach yourself to focus on the outside edges of your vision—It's called peripheral vision, like seeing something out of the corner of your eye. When you do that the vision in the middle, which you normally use to look at things, softens. That allows you to see the things that aren't obvious. Takes practice. Indians learn to do it when they're young, which is why they're so good at it."

Jim Bridger, Hugh could tell, wasn't sure whether to believe him or not.

"Just practice it whenever you get the chance and it'll happen. When it does, it'll seem so obvious you'll wonder how you never saw the tracks before."

"That," he added, "I can promise."

As he had tried to do in the past, Henry insisted that Hugh remain with the others in the party.

"Especially now," Henry told him, "with the danger of attack from every known tribe imminent, we have to stay together." He wanted a tight, compact group, with no strays or stragglers.

"I'm sorry, Major," Hugh told him. "Can't do it. Don't worry—I'll stay within earshot. If anything happens, I'll come running."

"And what if something happens to you?" Major Henry shot back.

"I'll take my chances."

Disgusted, Henry moved off.

Hugh was not about to change his mind. Too many times in the past, he had trusted his welfare to others. Too many times, that had almost proved to be his undoing. After spending nearly four years with the Pawnees, he found the movements of the whites to be clumsy and loud. Their lack of harmony in the wilderness spread out from them in all directions, like the ripples that were created when you threw a stone into a pond. The unnatural movements of birds and animals would telegraph the coming of the white men for anyone with eyes to see, just as the movements of the grass told of the coming of the wind. If anyone was in danger of detection here, it was they, and not Hugh Glass.

Besides that, he needed to be by himself today. His dreams had gotten him thinking about Little Feather again, and he wanted to be alone with her in his thoughts.

And that's exactly where he was when the

grizzly attacked…

Made in the USA
San Bernardino, CA
02 May 2018